GO TEAM!

EXTRA! EXTRA!
Replace the scattered hearts with dimensional paint or jewels.

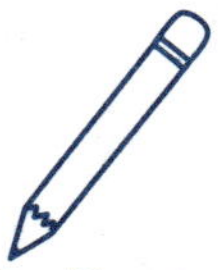
Test Transfer

Extra! Extra!

Add jewels or sequins to the dotted hearts and dimensional paint squiggles on the remaining hearts. Pom-pom flower centers would also look cute.

Test Transfer

EXTRA! EXTRA!

Use ribbons for borders by layering a dotted ribbon on top of a wider solid ribbon. Glitter paint brushed over a solid paint adds extra sparkle.

EXTRA! EXTRA!

Replace borders at the top and bottom with coordinating rickrack or ribbon. Cover the circles with small buttons or change the hearts to heart beads.

Test Transfer

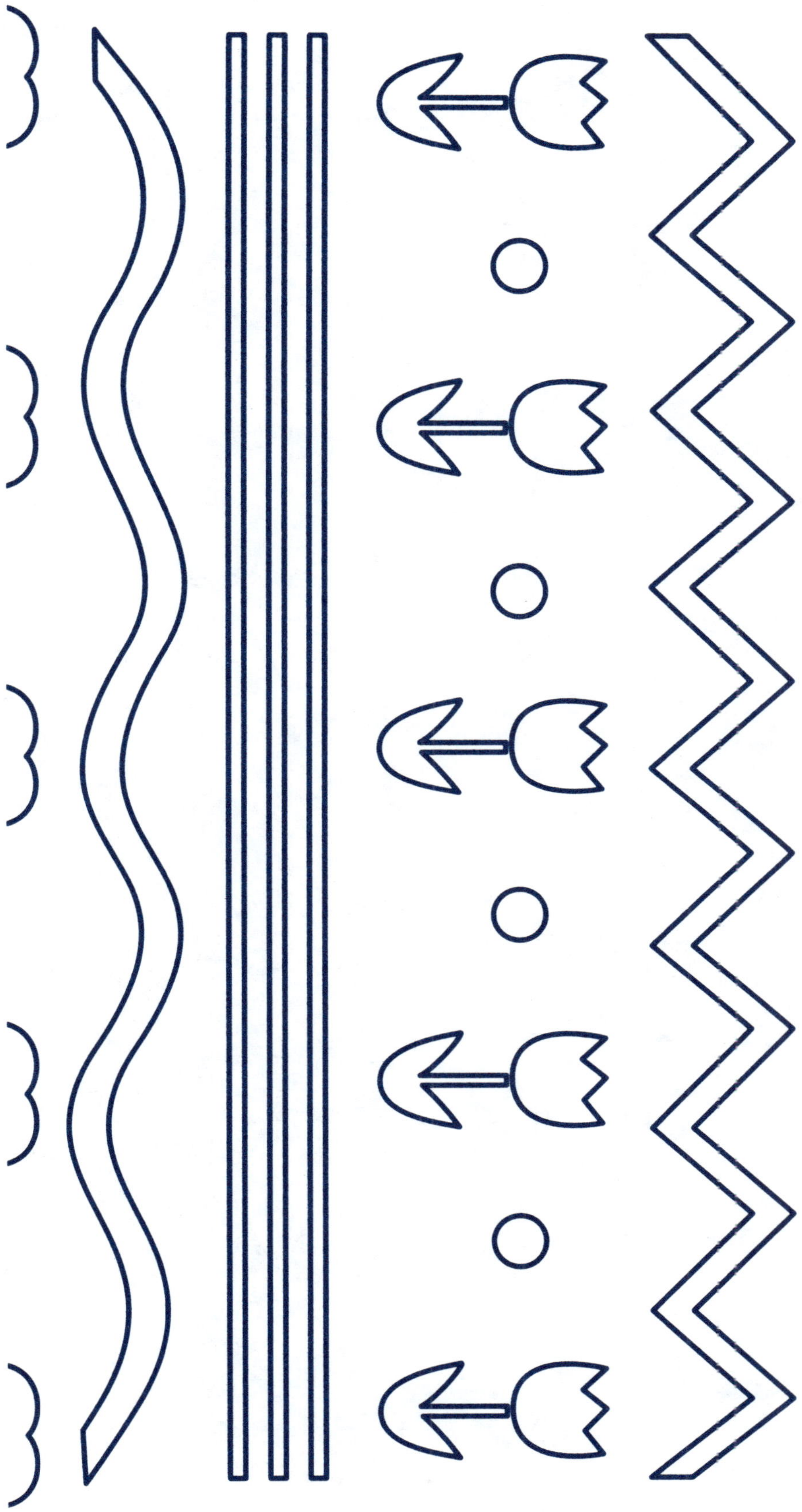

Extra! Extra!

Make this Easter egg special by adding round jewels and dimensional paint outlines and flower petals. Add rickrack to your T-shirt around the sleeves and bottom and sew on buttons and bows to complete the look.

Test Transfer

Extra! Extra!

Create a bang with starry and striped ribbons for the borders and the firecrackers. Add glitter paint and star jewels for more sparkle.

Test Transfer

EXTRA! EXTRA!

Make a Grand Old Flag by adding a patriotic ribbon border and glitter paint accents on the stars and stripes. Hold turned-up shirt sleeves in place with buttons.

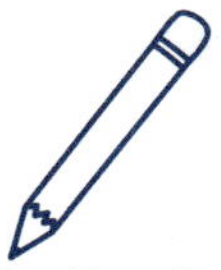

EXTRA! EXTRA!

Dress up the jack-o'-lanterns and cats with tiny ribbon bows. Place ribbon borders between each row. Dimensional paint, glow-in-the-dark fabric paint, or puffy paint will add to the spookiness of your design.

Test Transfer

EXTRA! EXTRA!
Let the witch silhouette fly across a harvest moon painted with glitter paint.

Extra! Extra!

Give our trio of witches personality by using curly ribbon for hair and tiny buttons for eyes. Dimensional paint or patterned ribbon livens up the brims of their hats.

Test Transfer

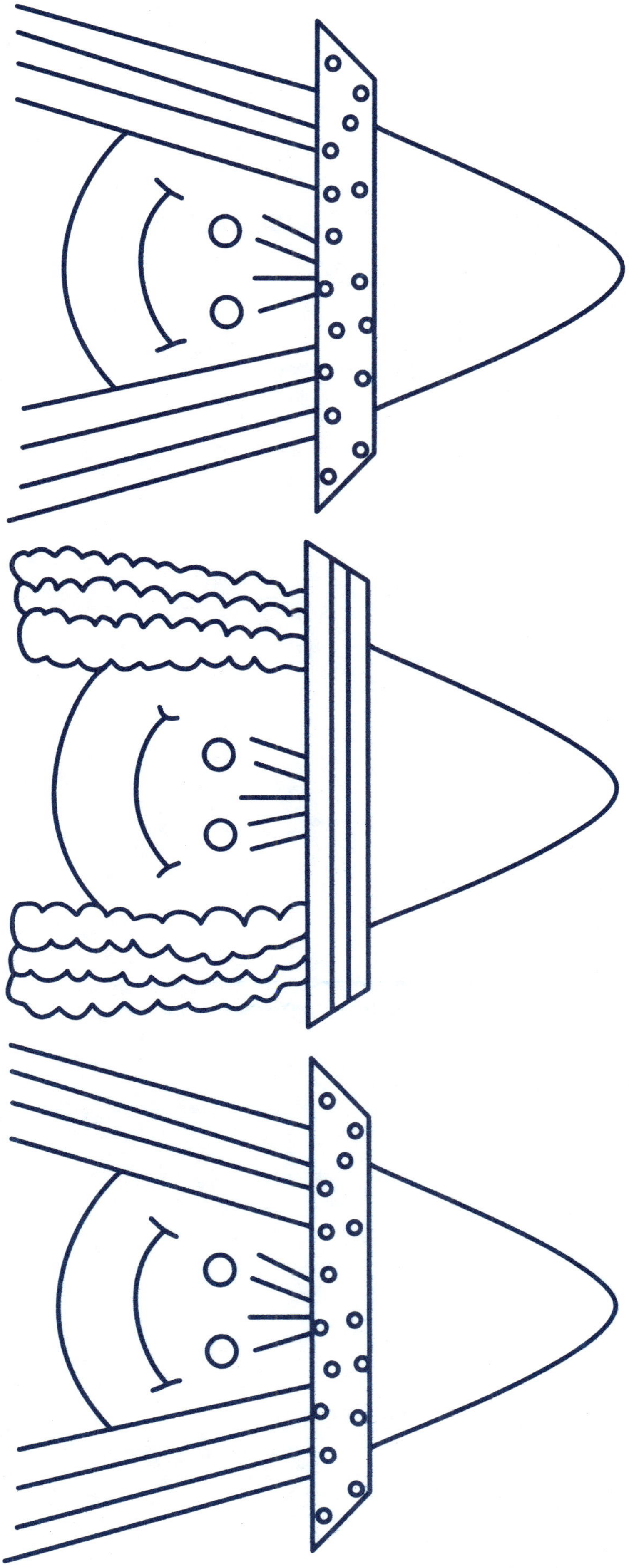

EXTRA! EXTRA!

A ribbon loop sewn on with a button makes a neat and easy leaf. For added sparkle, sprinkle gold glitter on dimensional paint outlines while they are wet.

Test Transfer

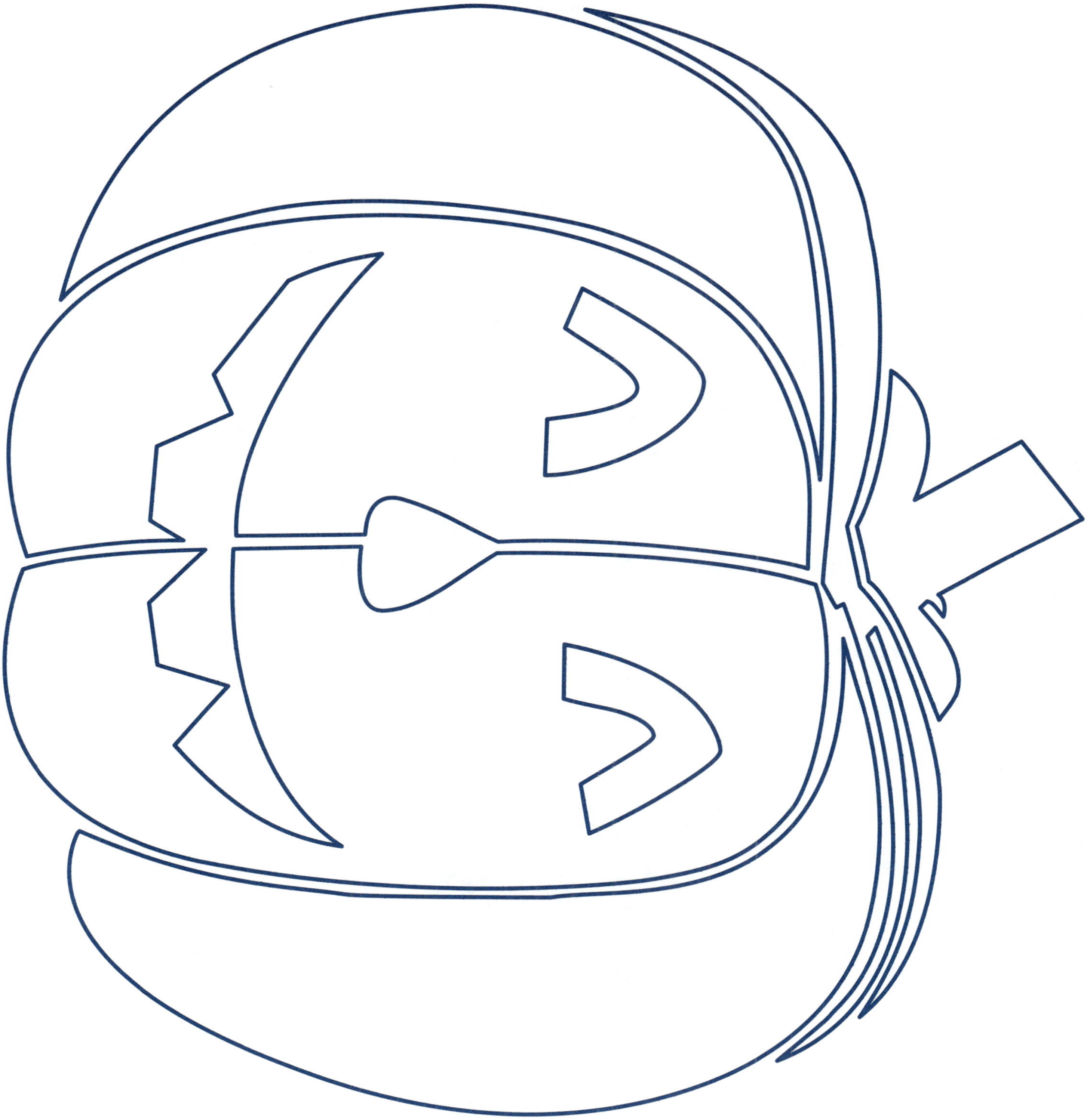

EXTRA! EXTRA!

Paint this pumpkin with puffy paint for a lifelike 3-D look.

Extra! Extra!

Use glow-in-the-dark fabric paint to paint a spooky ghost and replace the shutters with striped ribbon.

Test Transfer

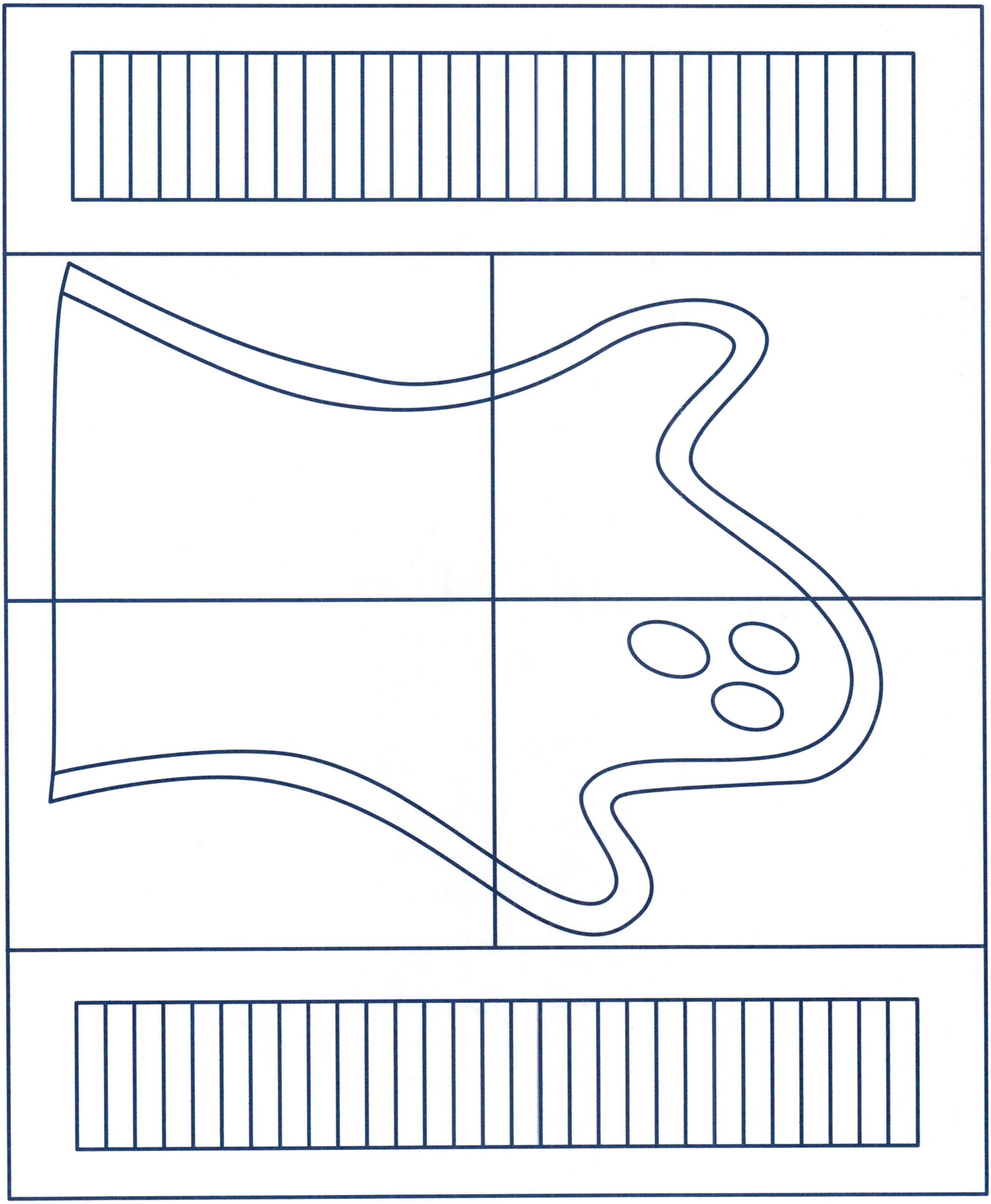

Extra! Extra!

Add some "bite" to the Count with a snappy ribbon bow tie, striped ribbon for pants, and satin ribbon to line his cape.

Test Transfer

Extra! Extra!

Use baby rickrack for instant wavy hair on this little witch. Add a bright ribbon hat brim, plaid ribbon shirt trim, and some freehand painted moons and stars for a quick finish.

Test Transfer

Extra! Extra!

Make dimensional tail feathers by folding wide lengths of ribbon to form points. Trim ribbon ends to fit along the turkey's body.

Extra! Extra!

Separate each row with a length of fall-colored ribbon. Folded ribbon can also be substituted for the turkeys' tail feathers.

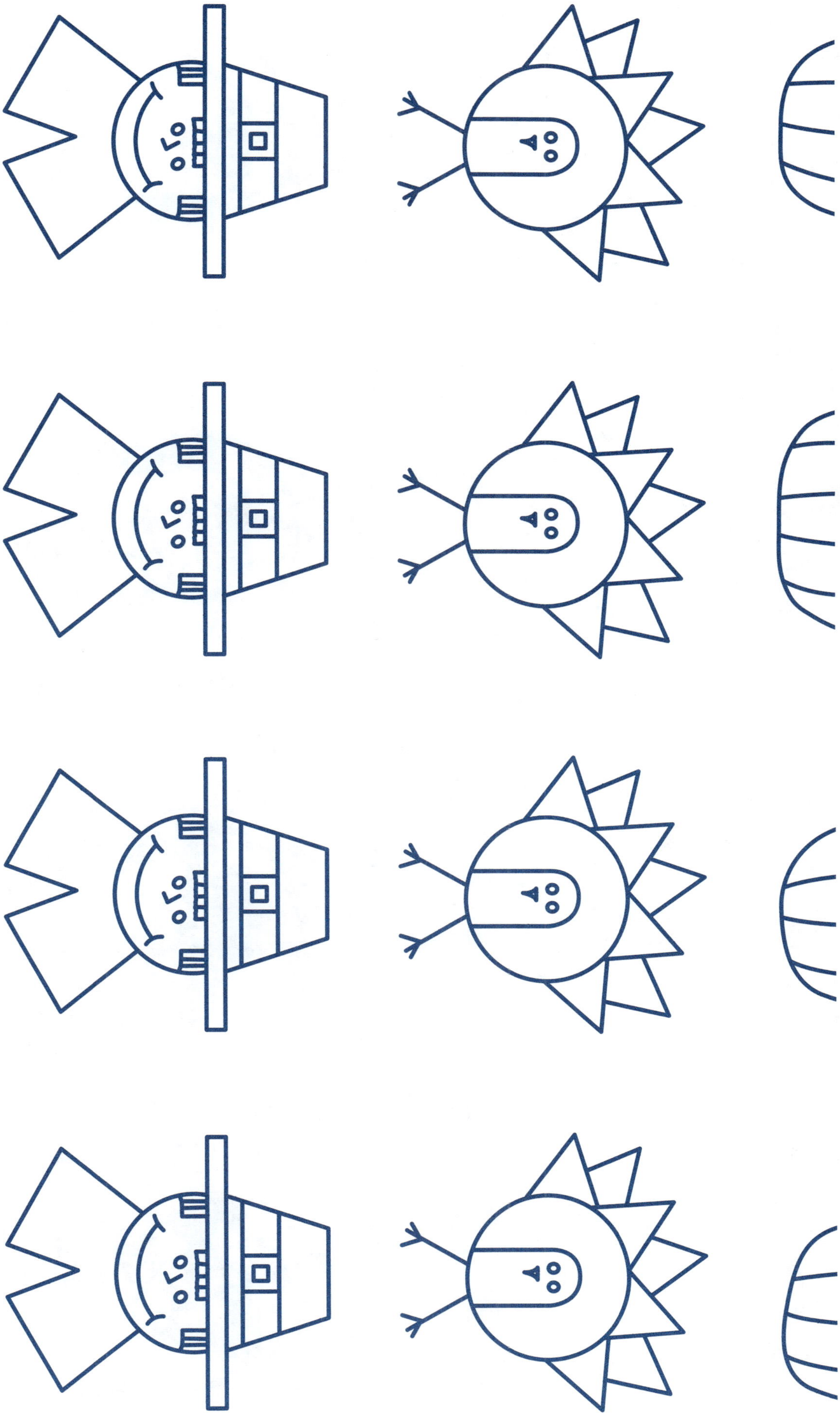

Test Transfer

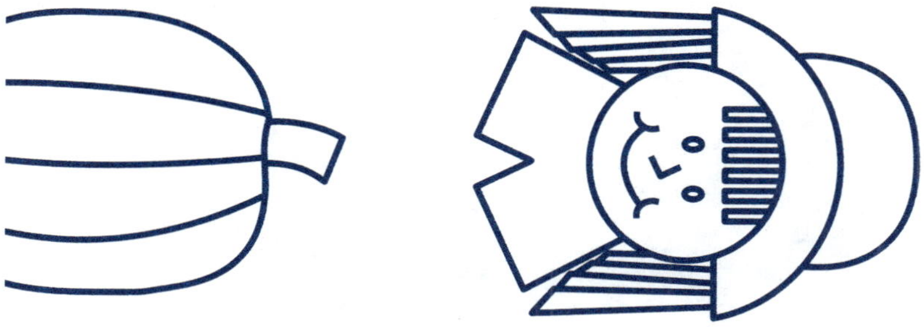

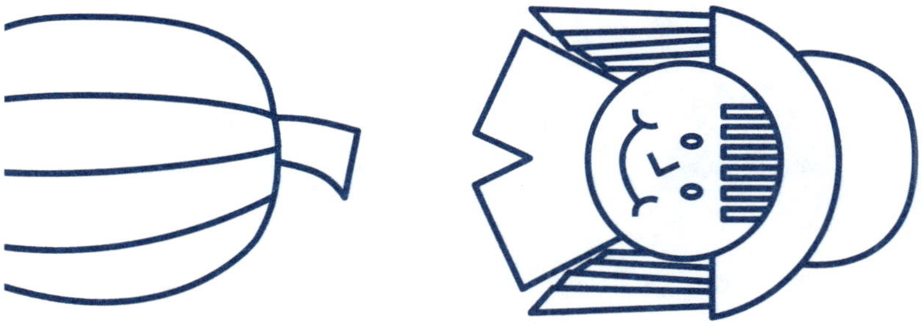

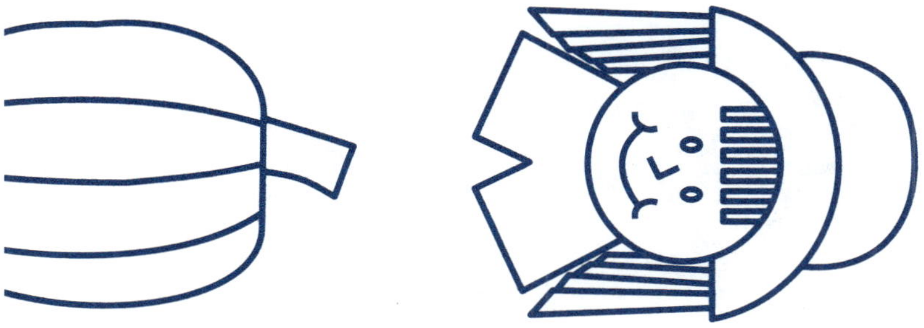

Extra! Extra!

Use a bold geometric ribbon for the border and for the girls' headbands. Dimensional paint for hair and buttons for eyes complete the look.

Test Transfer

EXTRA! EXTRA!

Let these three little boys peek above a border of solid ribbon layered on top of a wider ribbon.

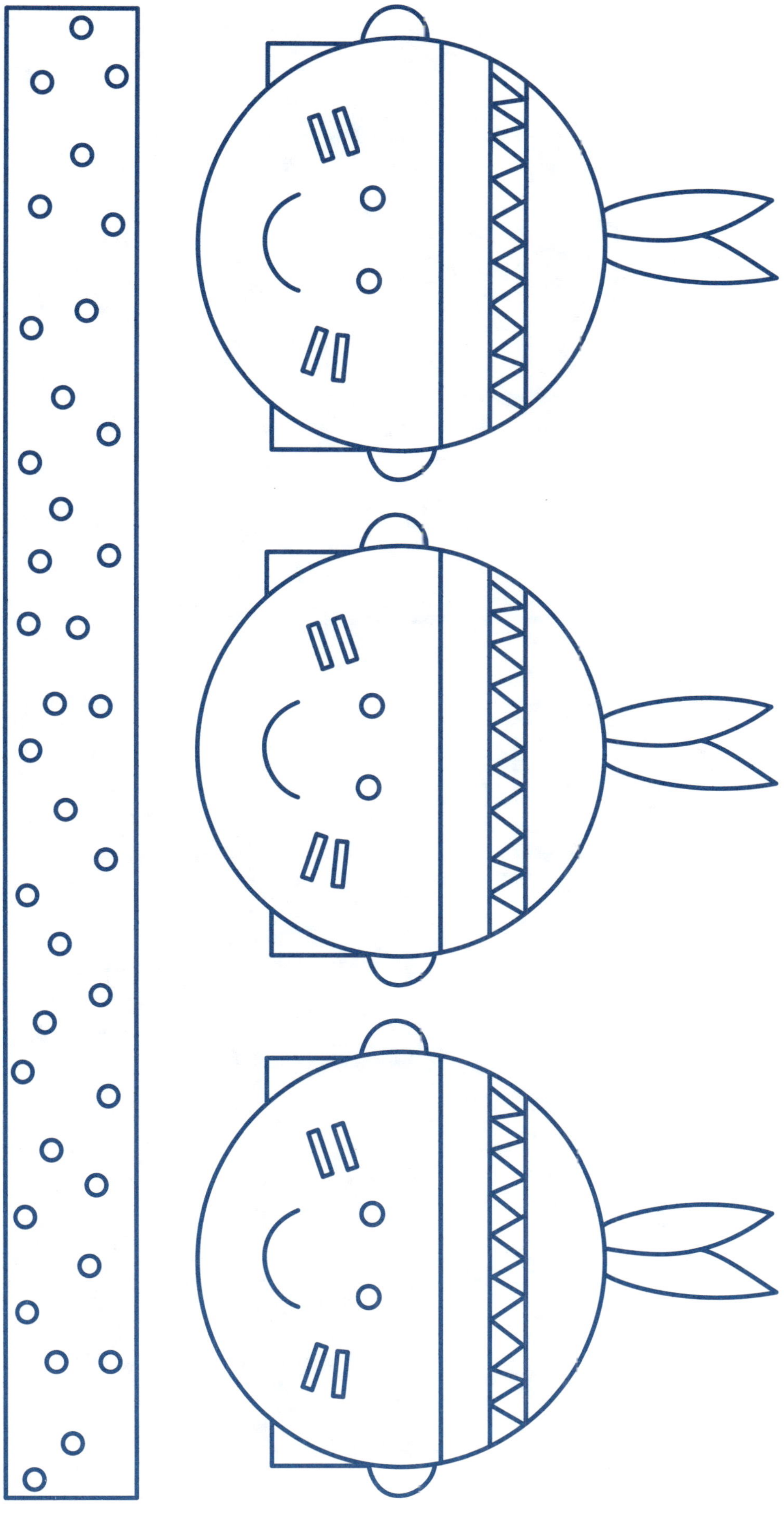

Extra! Extra!

Use varying widths of ribbon to make the snowman's hat and top it off by pinning an artificial flower in place. Knot a length of flannel fabric, fringe the ends, and pin it to the shirt to make a warm scarf.

Test Transfer

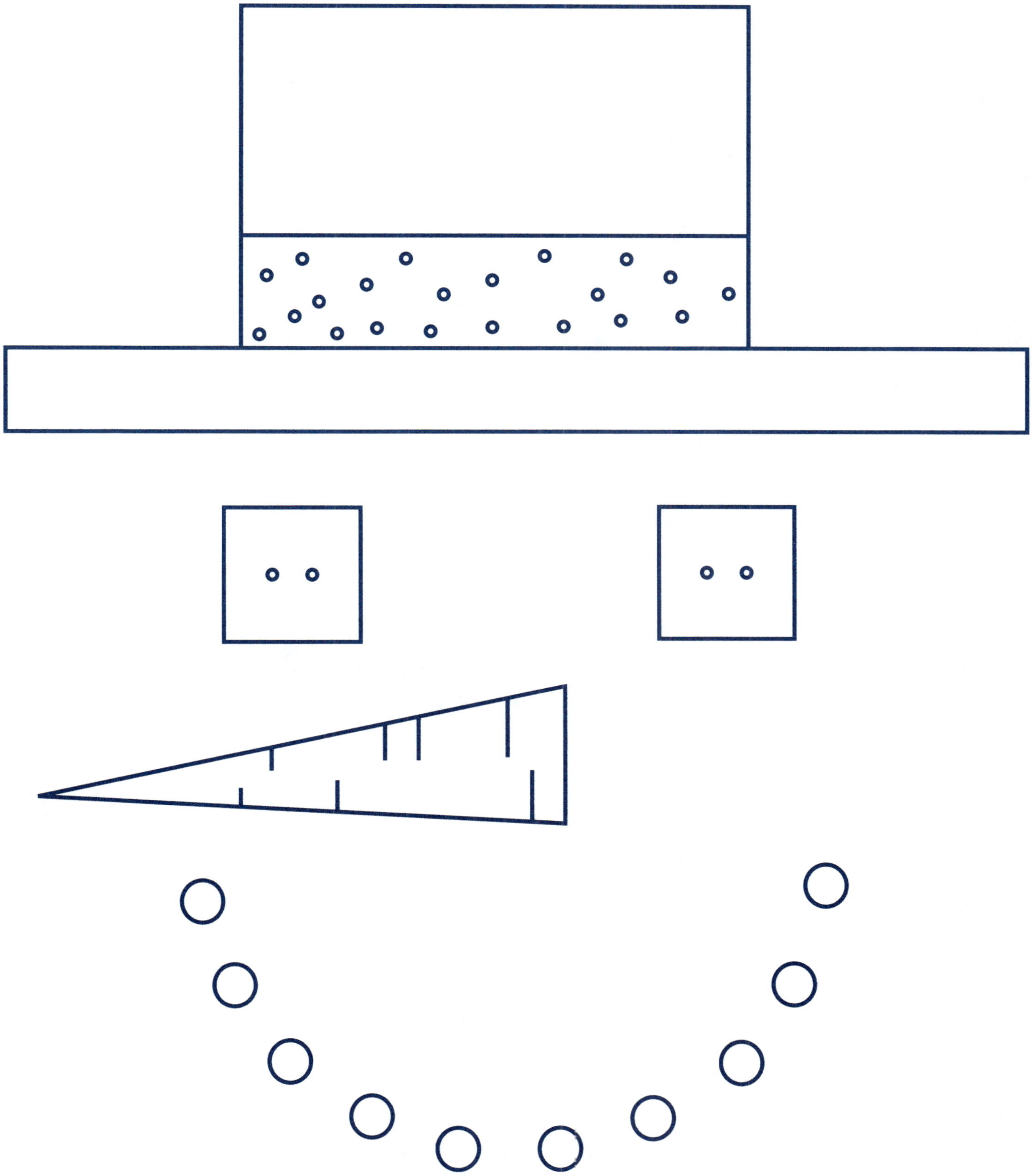

EXTRA! EXTRA!

Make the mitten strings out of real string, yarn, or ribbon! Add colorful pom-poms or buttons to replace the polka-dots.

Test Transfer

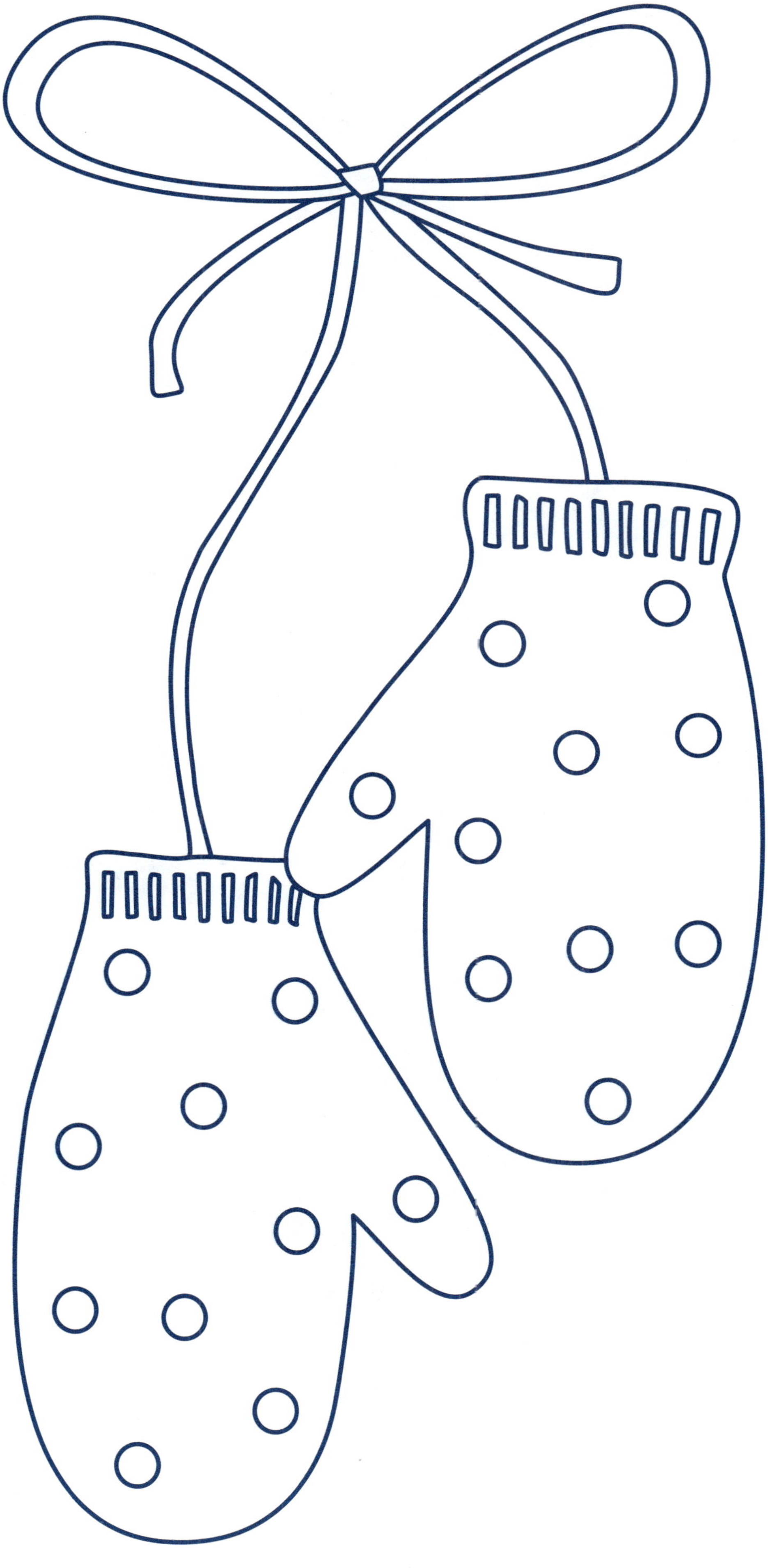

Extra! Extra!

Paint this design on a green shirt, then add rickrack borders and jeweled ornaments for a festive look.

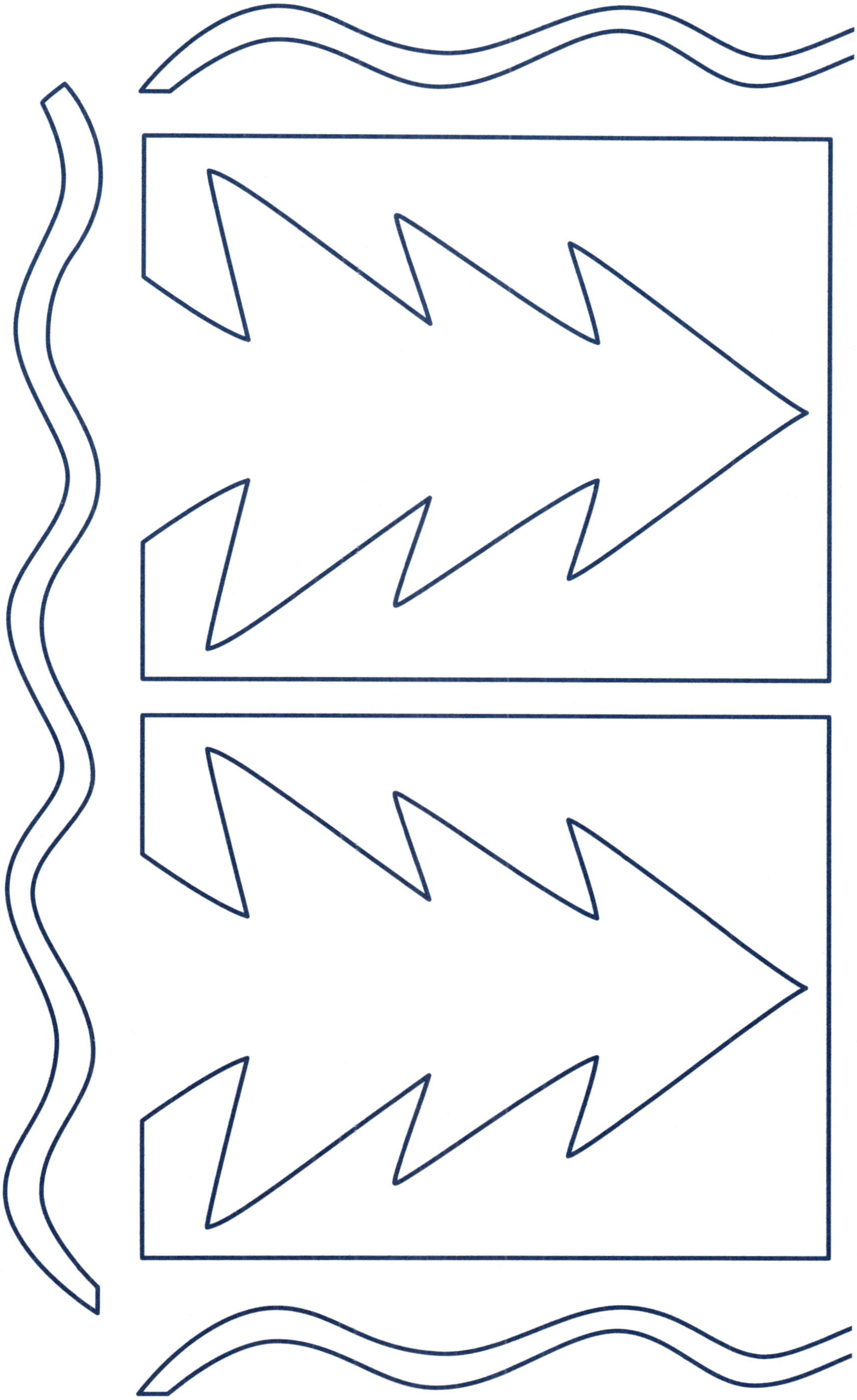

Test Transfer

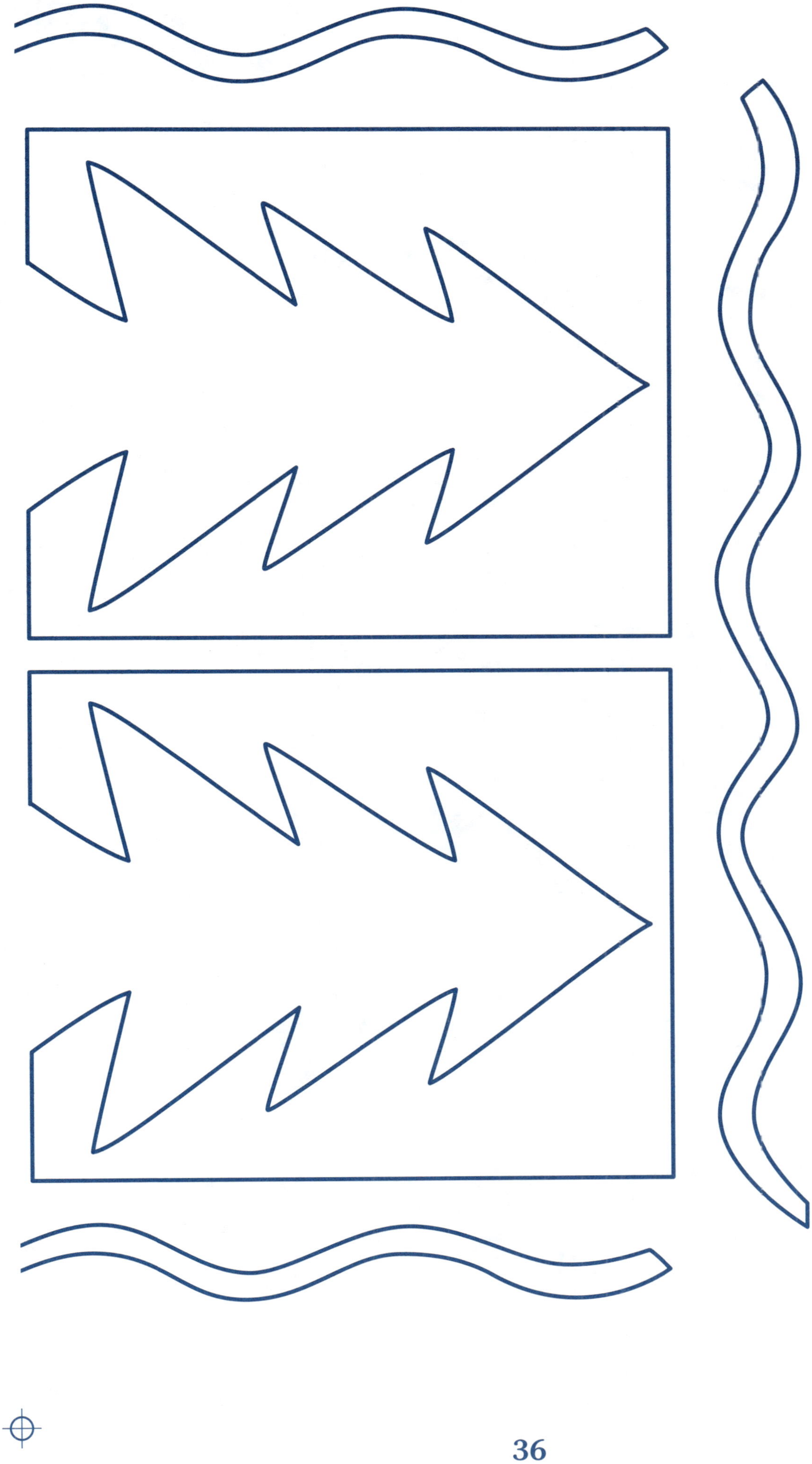

Extra! Extra!

Replace the stocking cuff with plaid ribbon. Add jewels to the wreath for sparkly "berries" and don't forget a real ribbon bow! Let the angel hold a star charm. Add holiday sparkle with glitter paint.

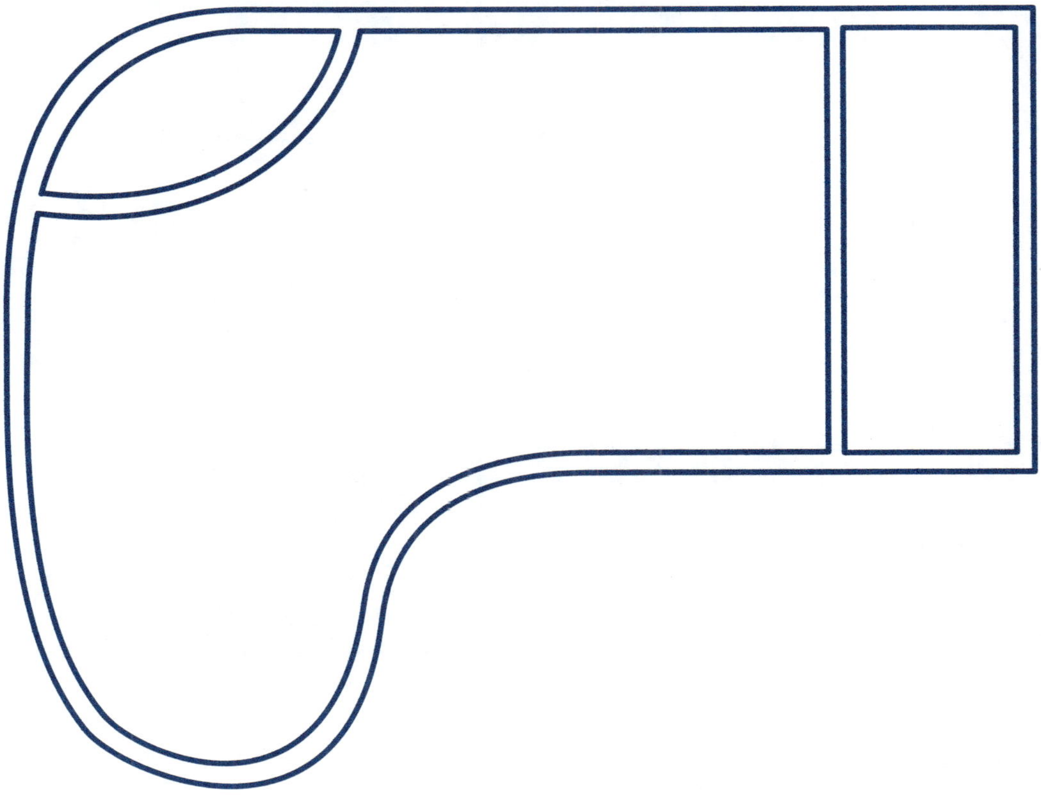

Extra! Extra!

Square buttons in red and green make a beautiful tree. Or, paint some squares green and add various colored buttons in remaining squares for ornaments. A Christmas ribbon border would also be pretty.

Test Transfer

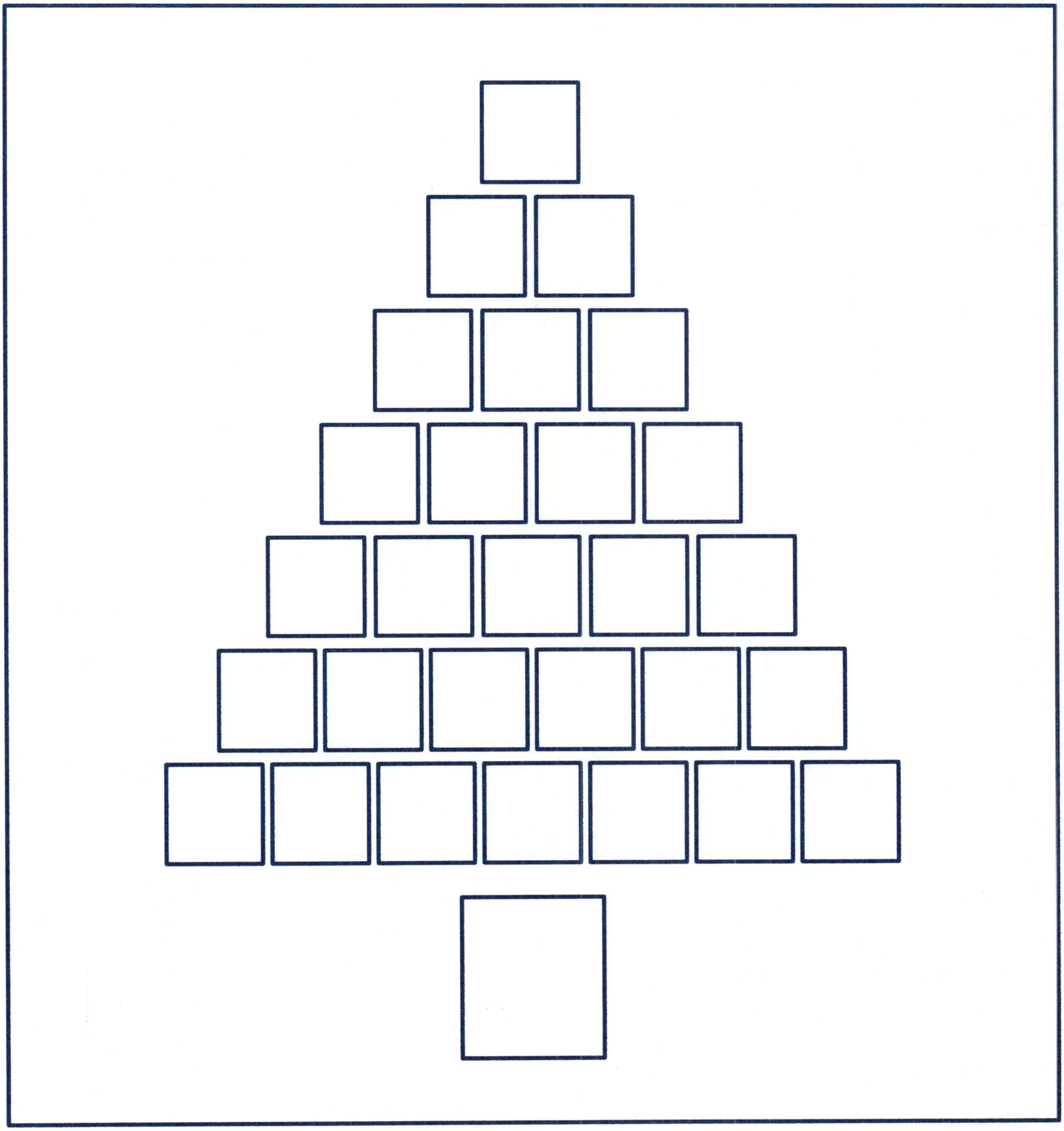

EXTRA! EXTRA!

Add gold star buttons or charms and bright ribbon outlines to these festive ties that are sized just right for father and son.

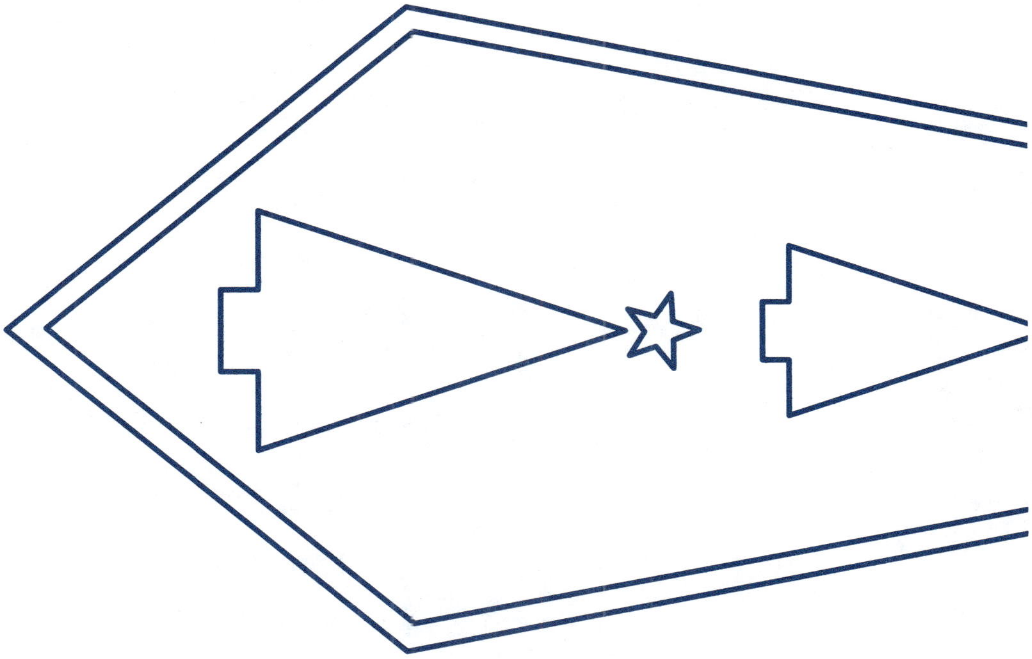

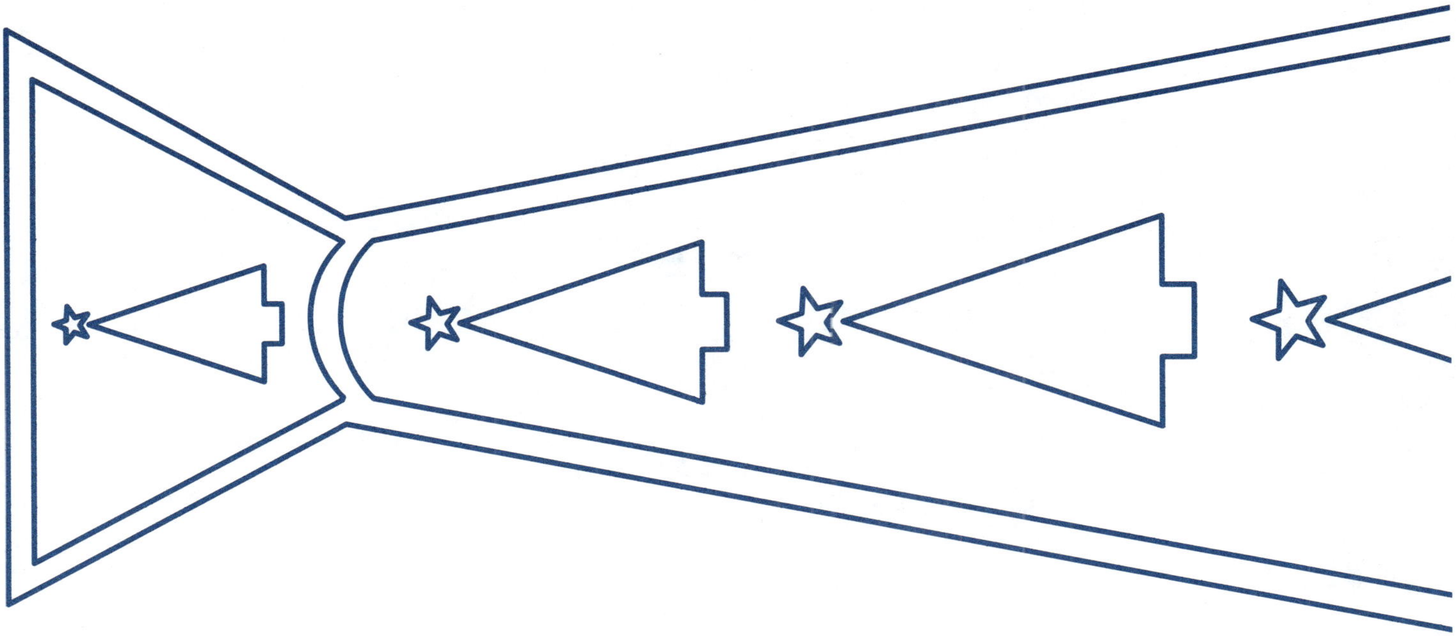

Test Transfer

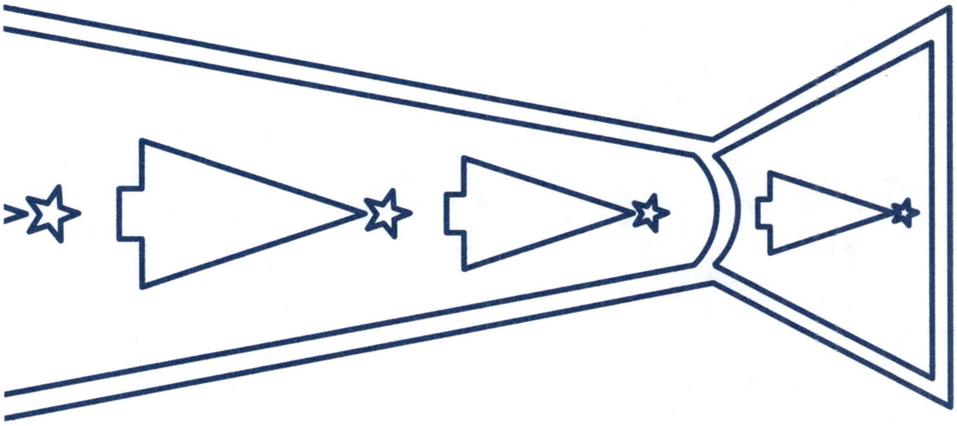

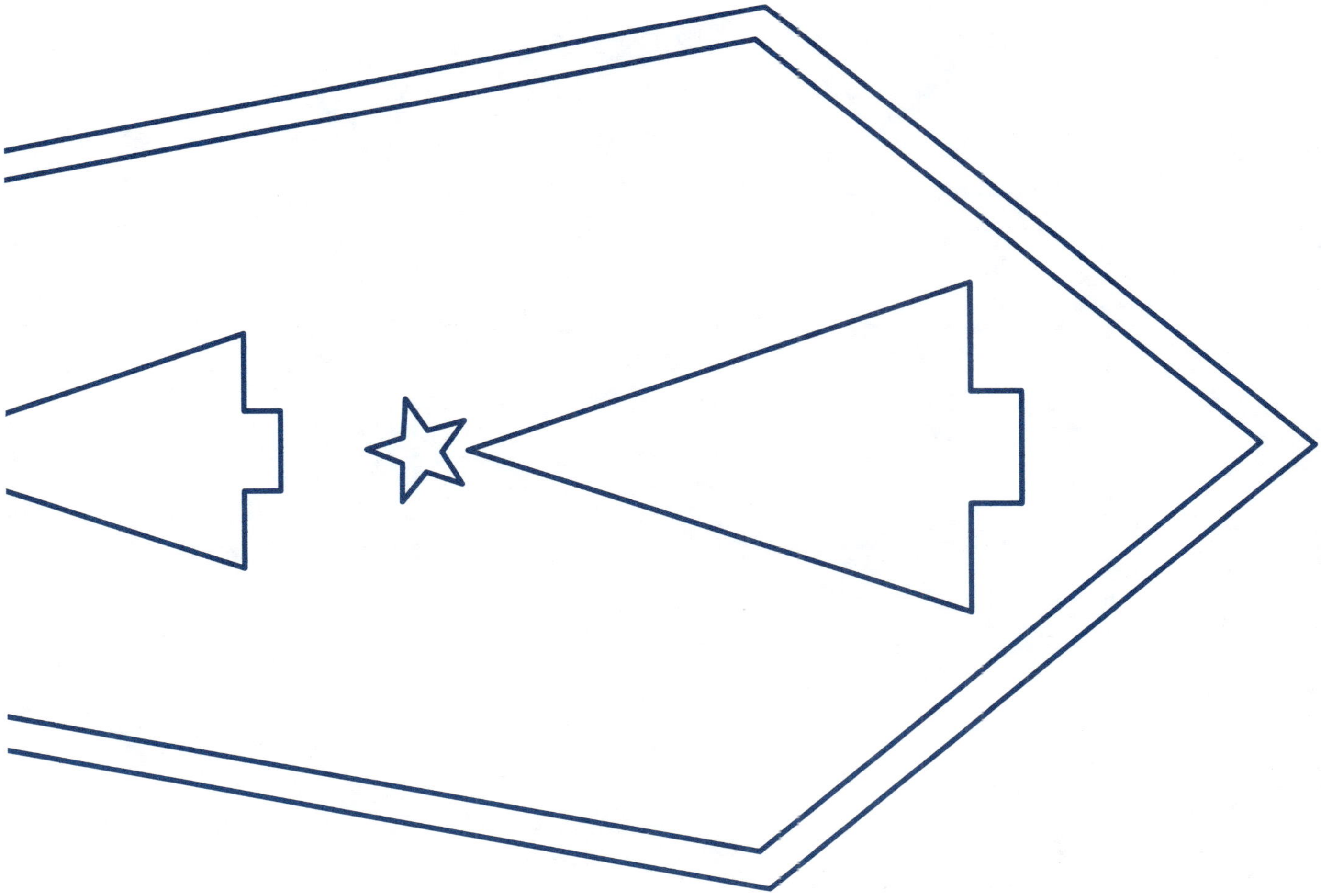

Extra! Extra!

Use a pom-pom for Santa's hat, dimensional glitter paint for the brim, cuffs, and whiskers, and ribbon on the chimney for an adorable shirt with holiday spirit.

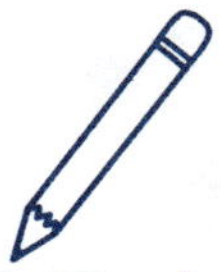

Test Transfer

Extra! Extra!

Add jewels or dimensional paint to the packages and then top them with bows tied from ribbon.

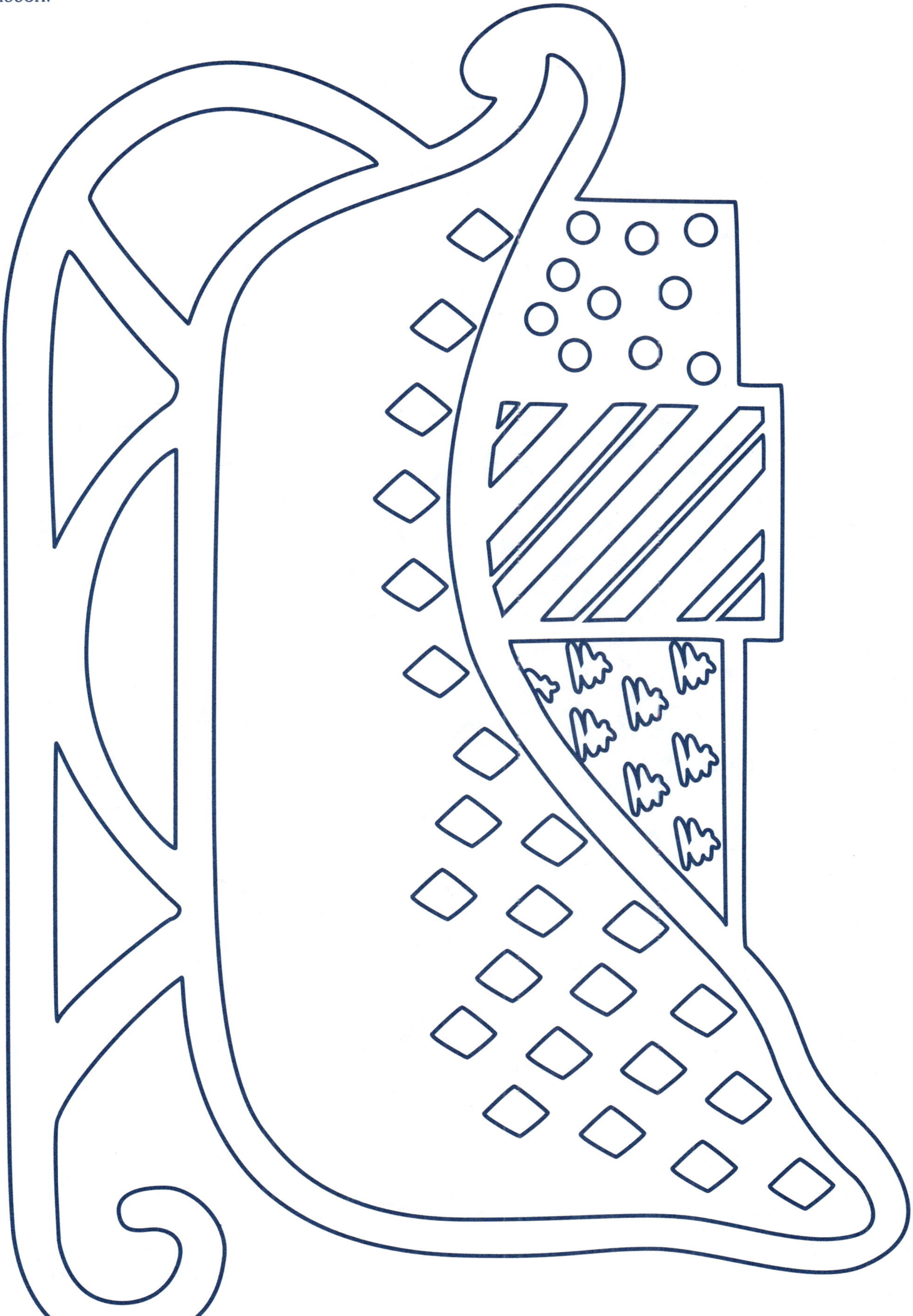

Extra! Extra!

Use gold metallic rickrack or braid for his hatband and coat trim. Add some gold metallic fringe sewn or glued to his shoulders for the epaulets.

Test Transfer

Extra! Extra!

Sprinkle fine glitter on dimensional paint while it is still wet for a fresh-fallen snow look. Use dimensional paint to add jewels, then pin on ribbon bows for a finishing touch!

Test Transfer

EXTRA! EXTRA!

Use this large design on a wall hanging or nightshirt. Use polka-dot ribbon to make each of the H's and tie a festive ribbon bow to each of the wreath O's.

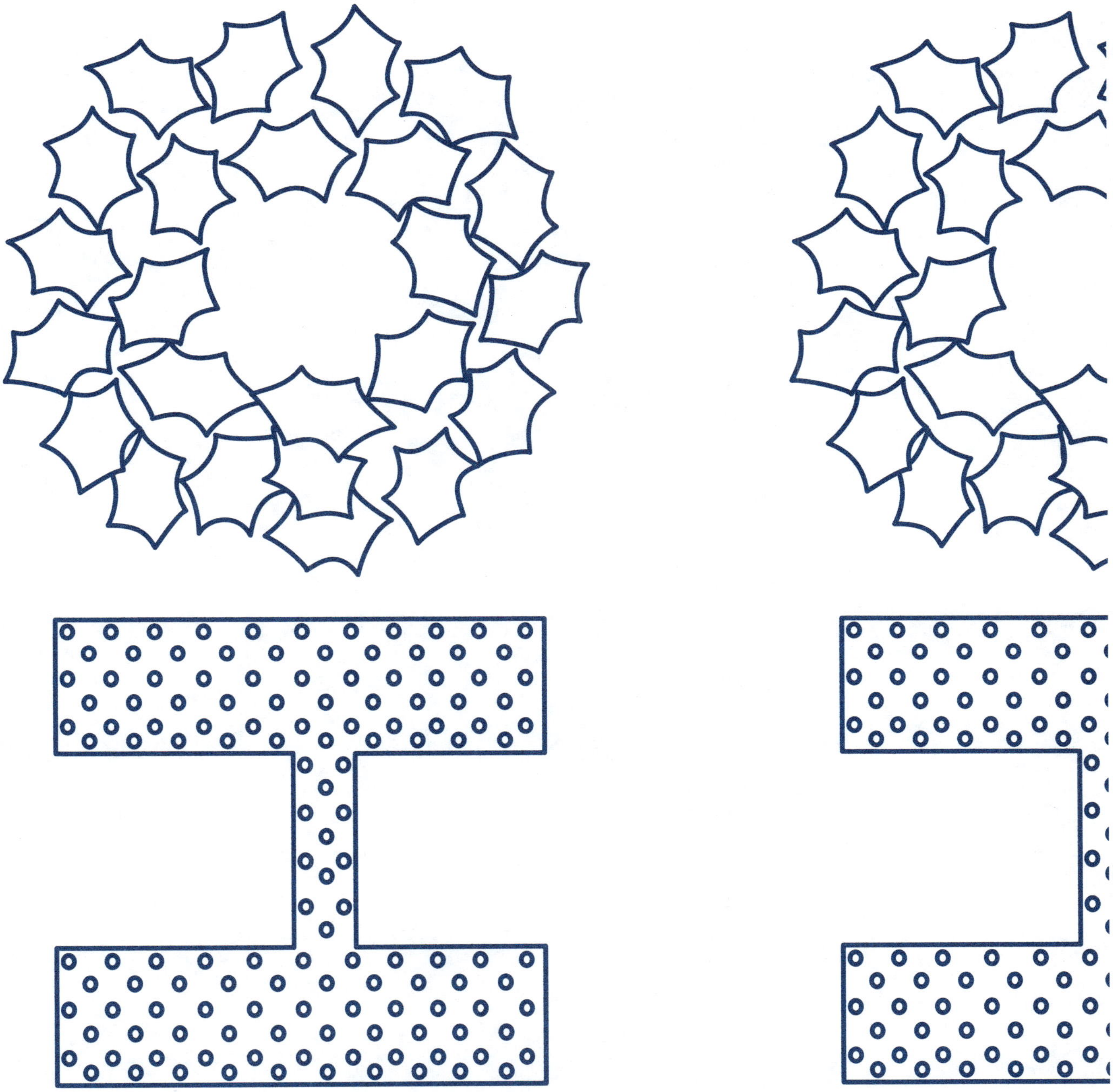

Test Transfer

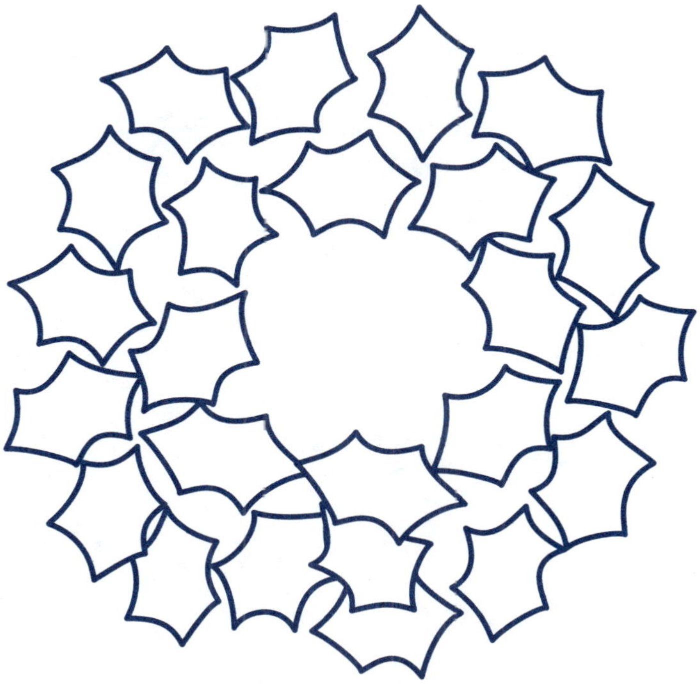

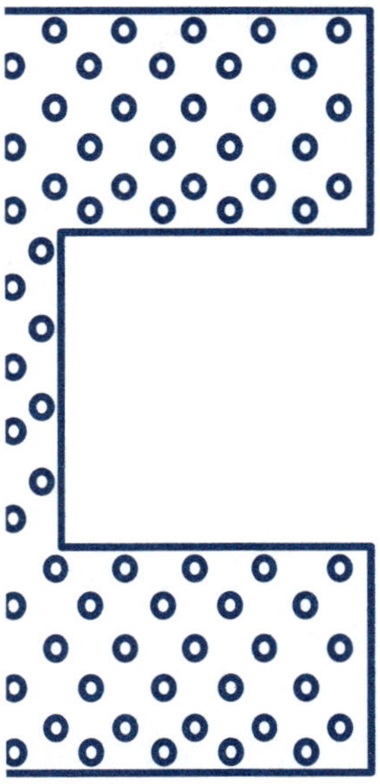

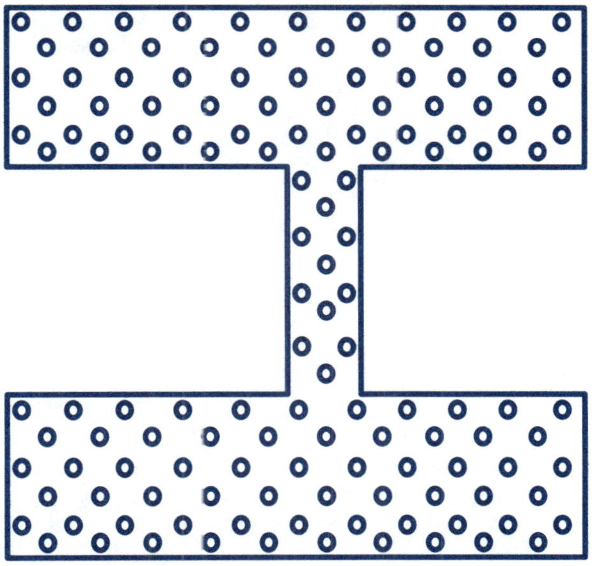

EXTRA! EXTRA!

Use ribbon to form H's, then add glitter paint and jewels for extra sparkle.

EXTRA! EXTRA!

Add a ribbon border, buttons to the dresses, and dimensional paint or curly ribbon for hair to this celestial trio.

EXTRA! EXTRA!

Paint and embellish this heavenly angel with dimensional paint and very fine glitter for a look that's heaven sent.

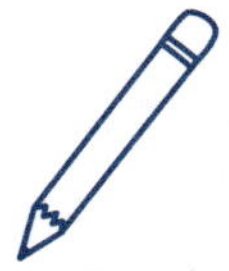

Test Transfer

EXTRA! EXTRA!

Celebrate those milestone birthdays (10, 20, 30, or 40) by transferring the desired number of candles to a shirt. Embellish with rickrack and jewels. Add a personal message to your creation using one of the alphabets given on pgs. 163-165.

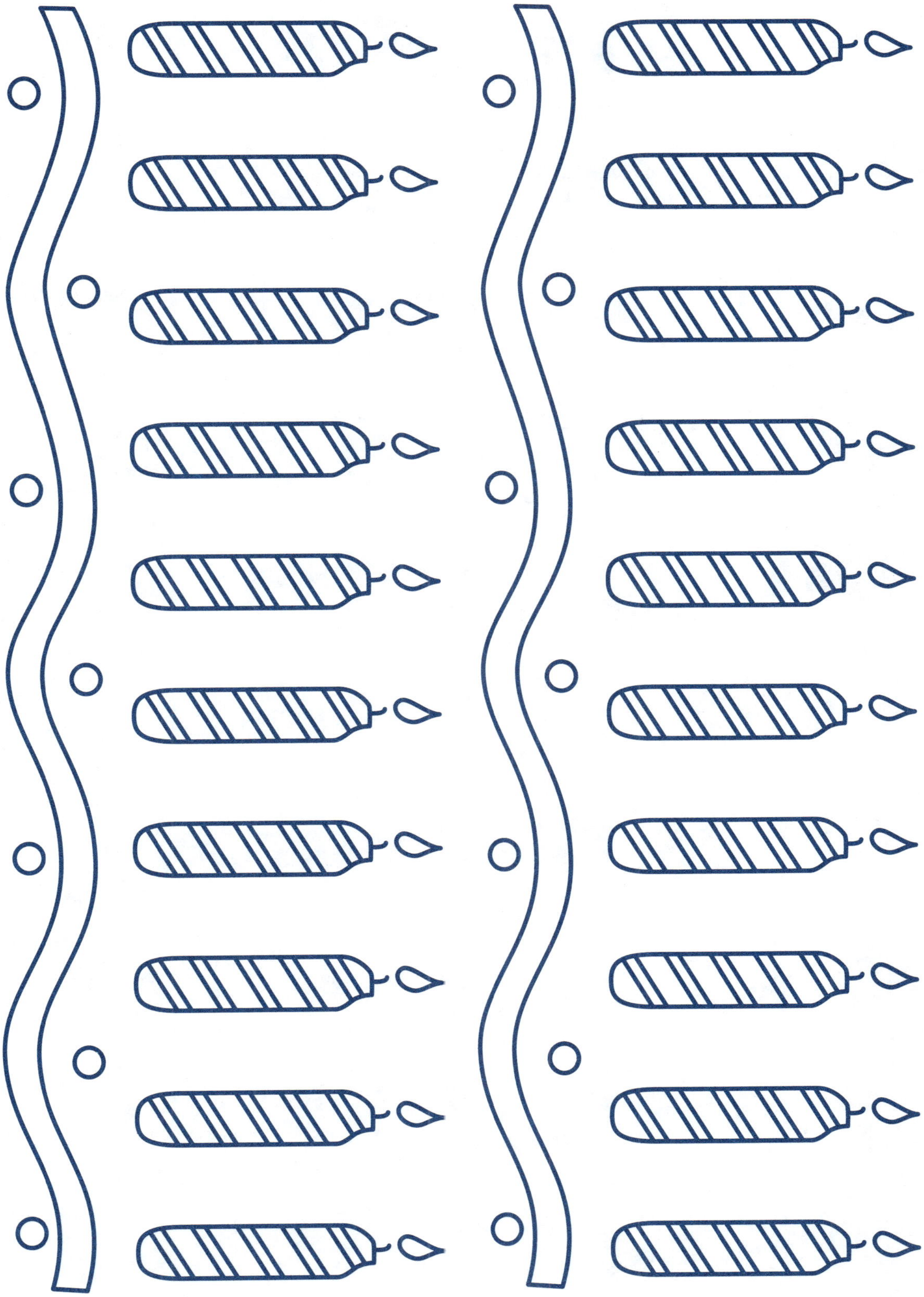

Test Transfer

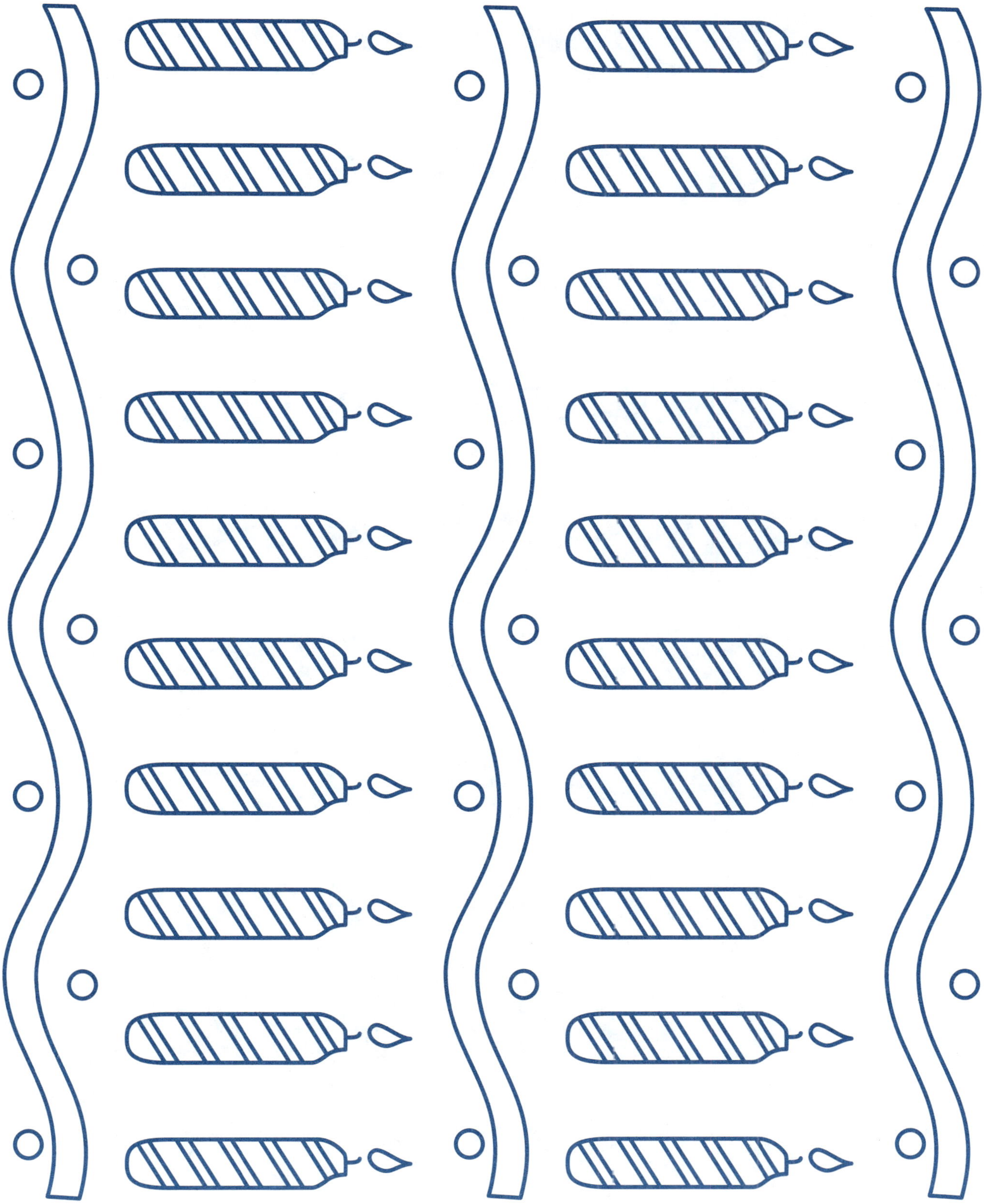

EXTRA! EXTRA!

Add or trim away as many candles as you like to make this birthday cupcake! Use dimensional paint for the sprinkles and pear-shaped jewels for the candle flames. Lace, buttons, and bows complement this cute design.

EXTRA! EXTRA!

Adding beads or dimensional paint sprinkles, a ribbon border, and 1/8"w ribbon on the cone keep this ice cream from melting all summer.

Test Transfer

EXTRA! EXTRA!

Dimensional paint or rattail cord for swirls and ribbon for sticks will make these lollipops yummy.

Test Transfer

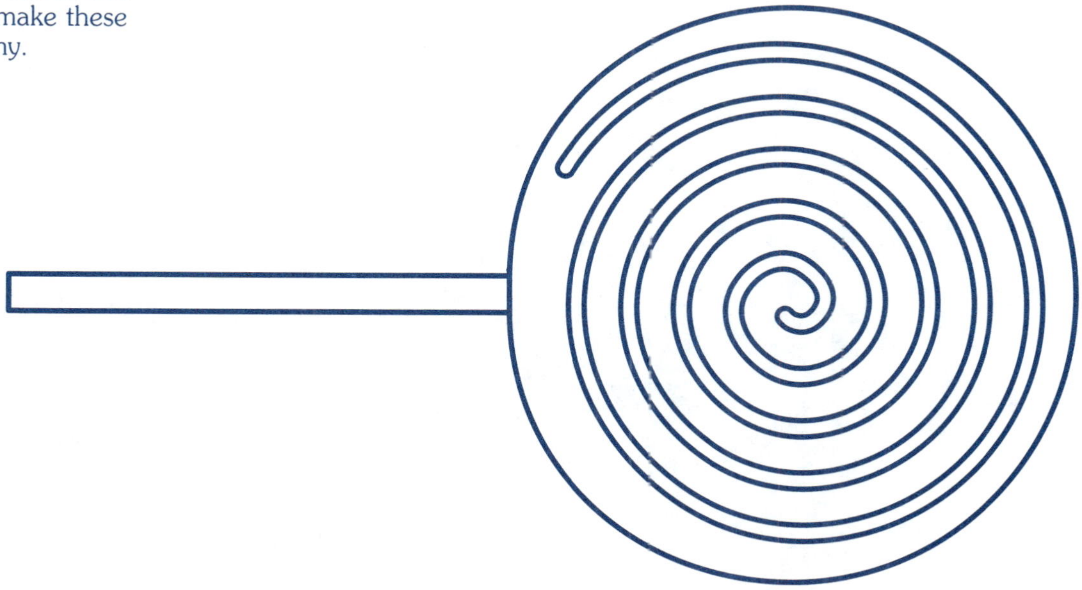

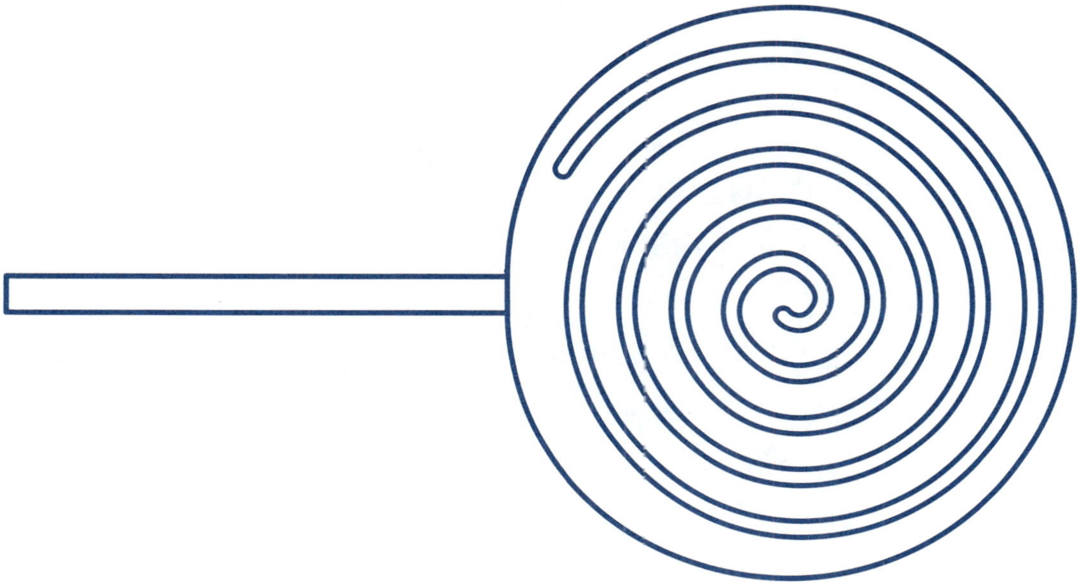

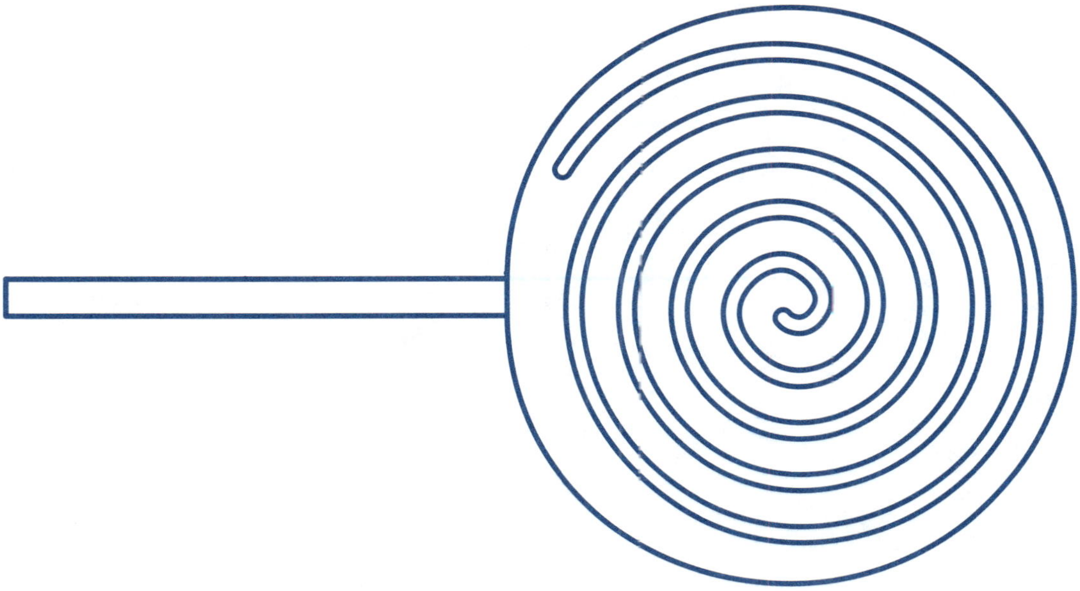

Extra! Extra!

Enhance this birthday design with lots of shiny dimensional paint and bright balloon buttons.

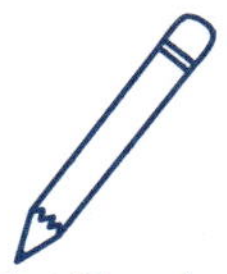

Test Transfer

Extra! Extra!

Make your birthday boy happy with lots of bright colors and dimensional paint.

Test Transfer

EXTRA! EXTRA!

Highlight the confetti and pencil designs with dimensional paint, sequins, or various-shaped jewels.

Test Transfer

Extra! Extra!

Replace this happy clown's eyes with buttons, his nose with a pom-pom, and outline him with dimensional paint. Cut a flower out of washable felt and use a button for the center or replace flower on hat with a flower button. Add rickrack around the edges of his collar.

Test Transfer

EXTRA! EXTRA!

Make a piñata from this pony by using curly ribbon or a tassel for the tail, a button for the eye, and colorful ribbon for the stripes.

Test Transfer

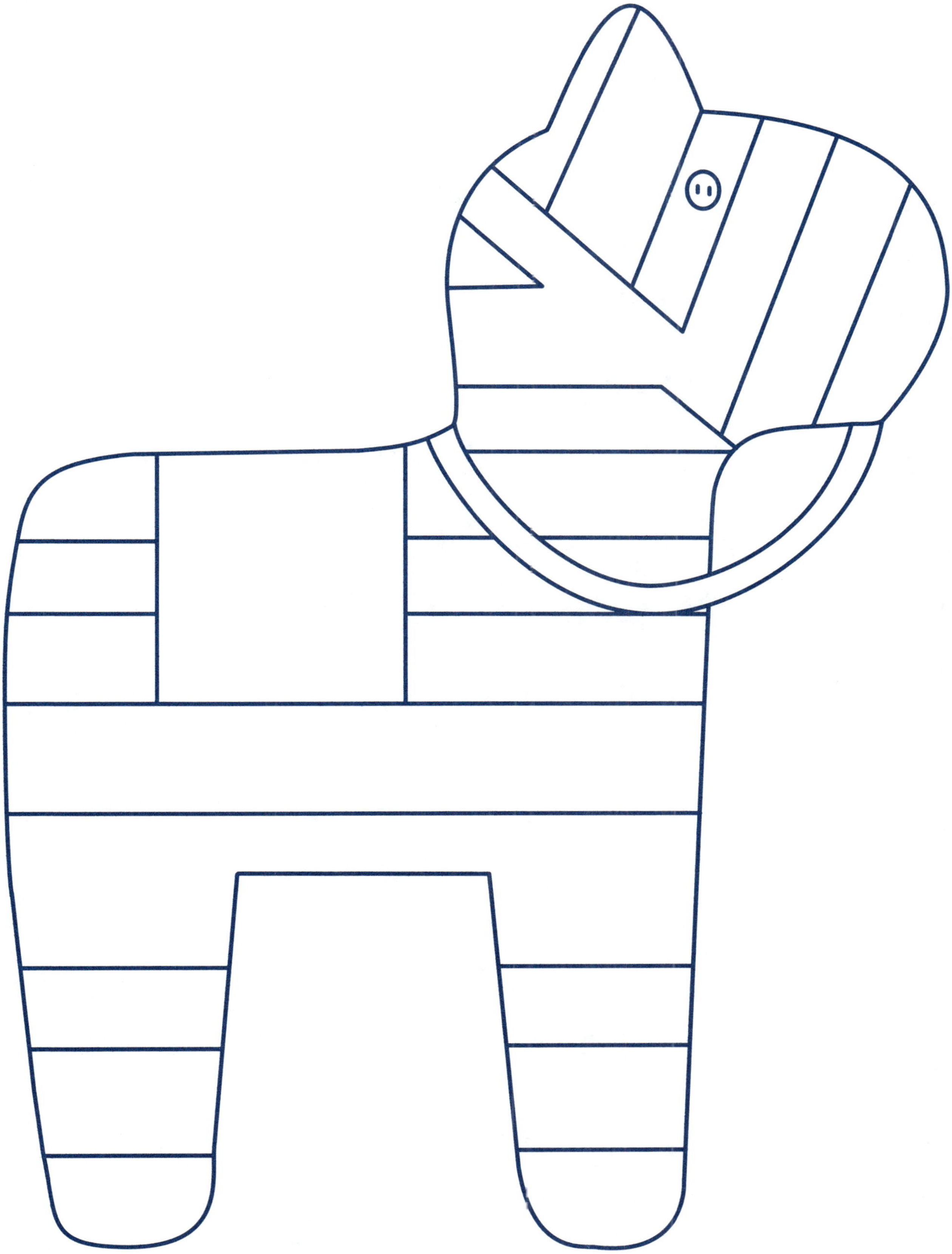

EXTRA! EXTRA!

Add lots of rickrack and sequins to brighten this festive design.

Extra! Extra!

Sew pom-poms to the daisy centers and outline with thick lines of dimensional paint for a unique look.

Test Transfer

EXTRA! EXTRA!

Use dimensional paint to outline and add dots, sew on buttons for the daisy centers, and add ribbon and rickrack borders for a cheery design.

Test Transfer

EXTRA! EXTRA!

Use seed beads or dimensional paint for flower centers, then add a ribbon bow for a fresh daisy look.

Test Transfer

Extra! Extra!

Replace the seeds on each berry with a seed bead or dimensional paint, then add a rickrack and ribbon border.

EXTRA! EXTRA!

Use rickrack to separate the pulp and the rind. Jewels, beads, or buttons work well for the seeds.

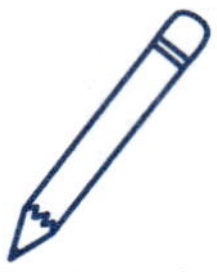

Test Transfer

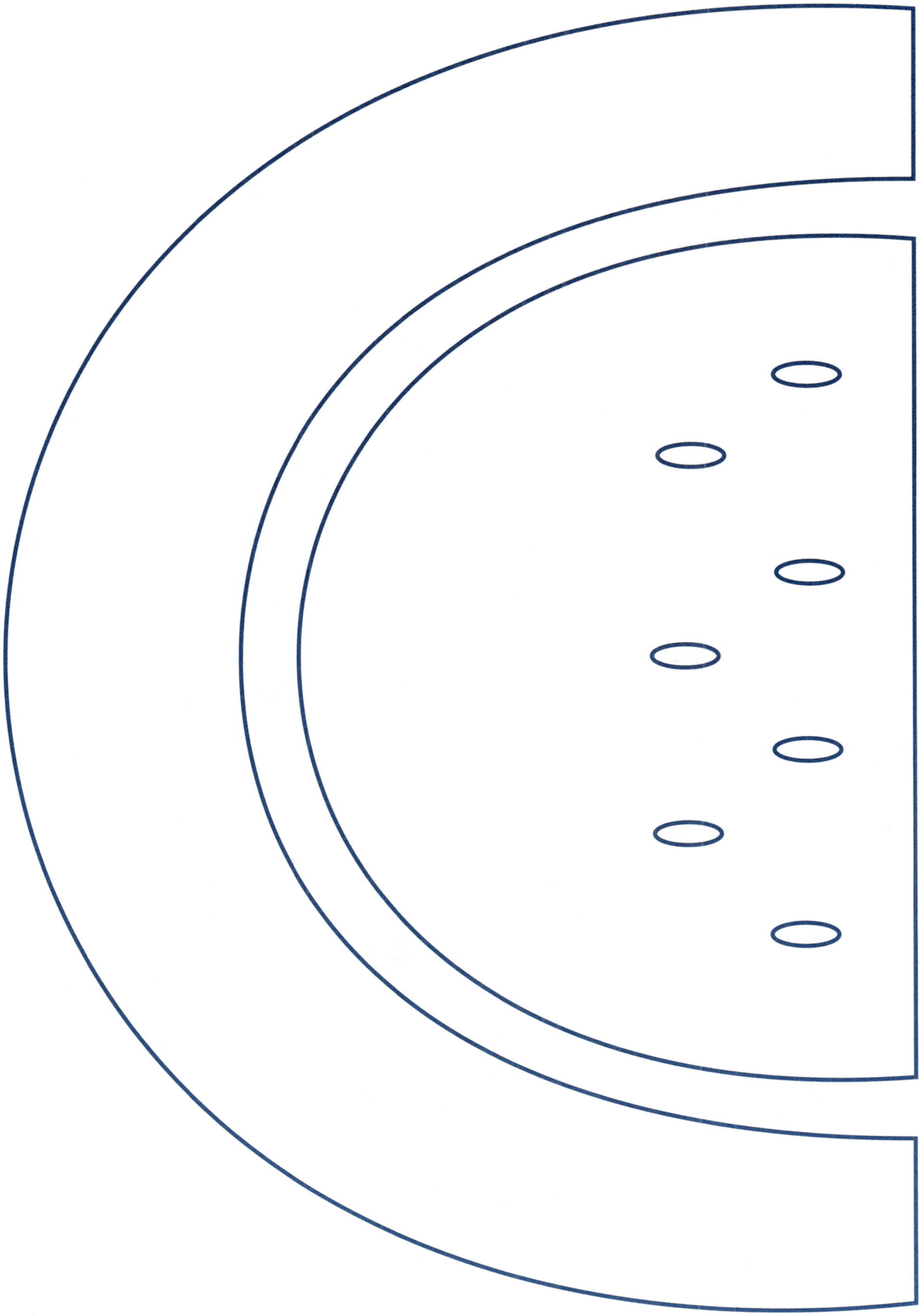

EXTRA! EXTRA!

Make carrot tops from lengths of ribbon, then add buttons for peas and dimensional paint outlines.

Test Transfer

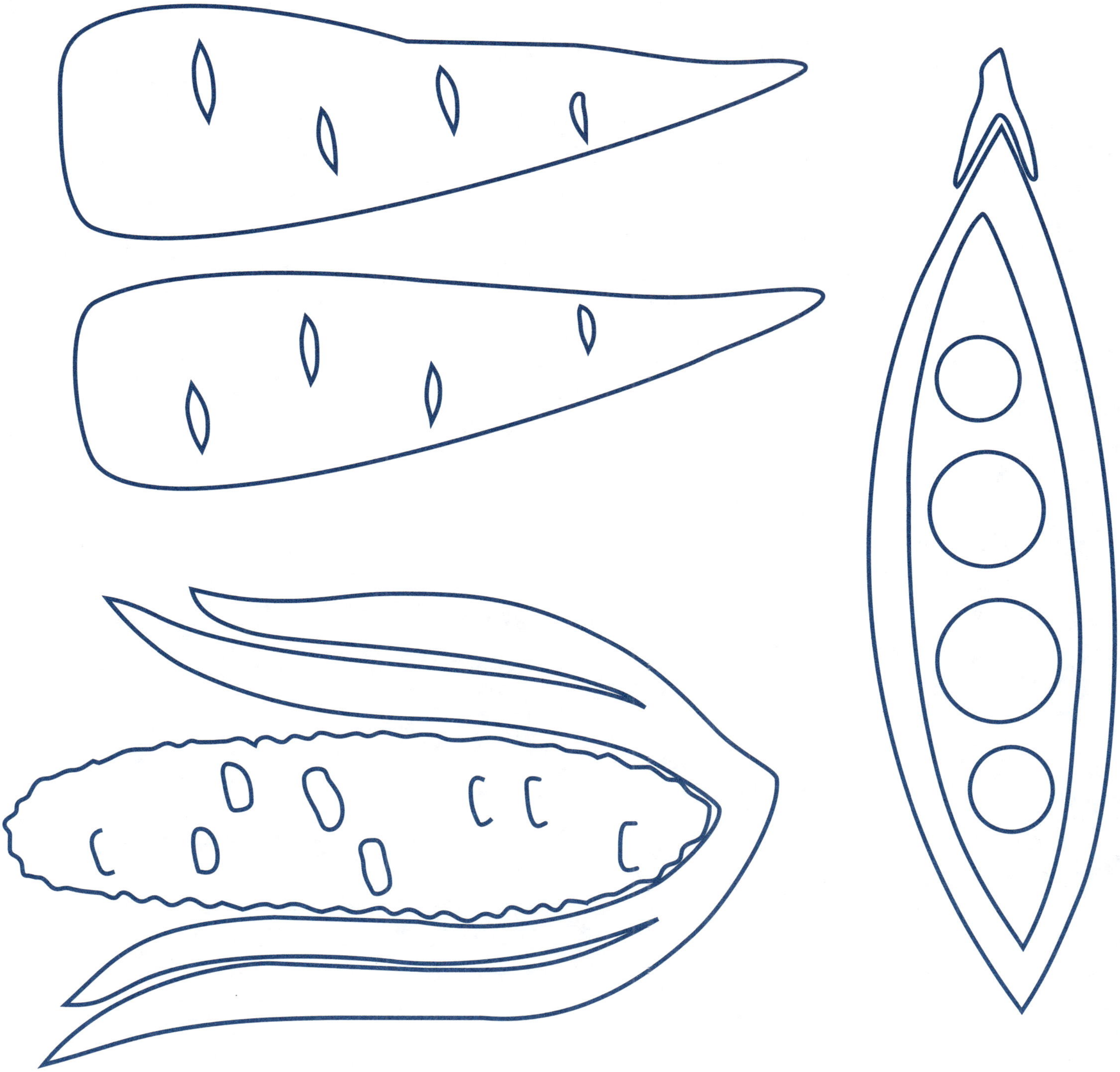

EXTRA! EXTRA!

Replace the borders with rickrack and use folded ribbon for the stems.

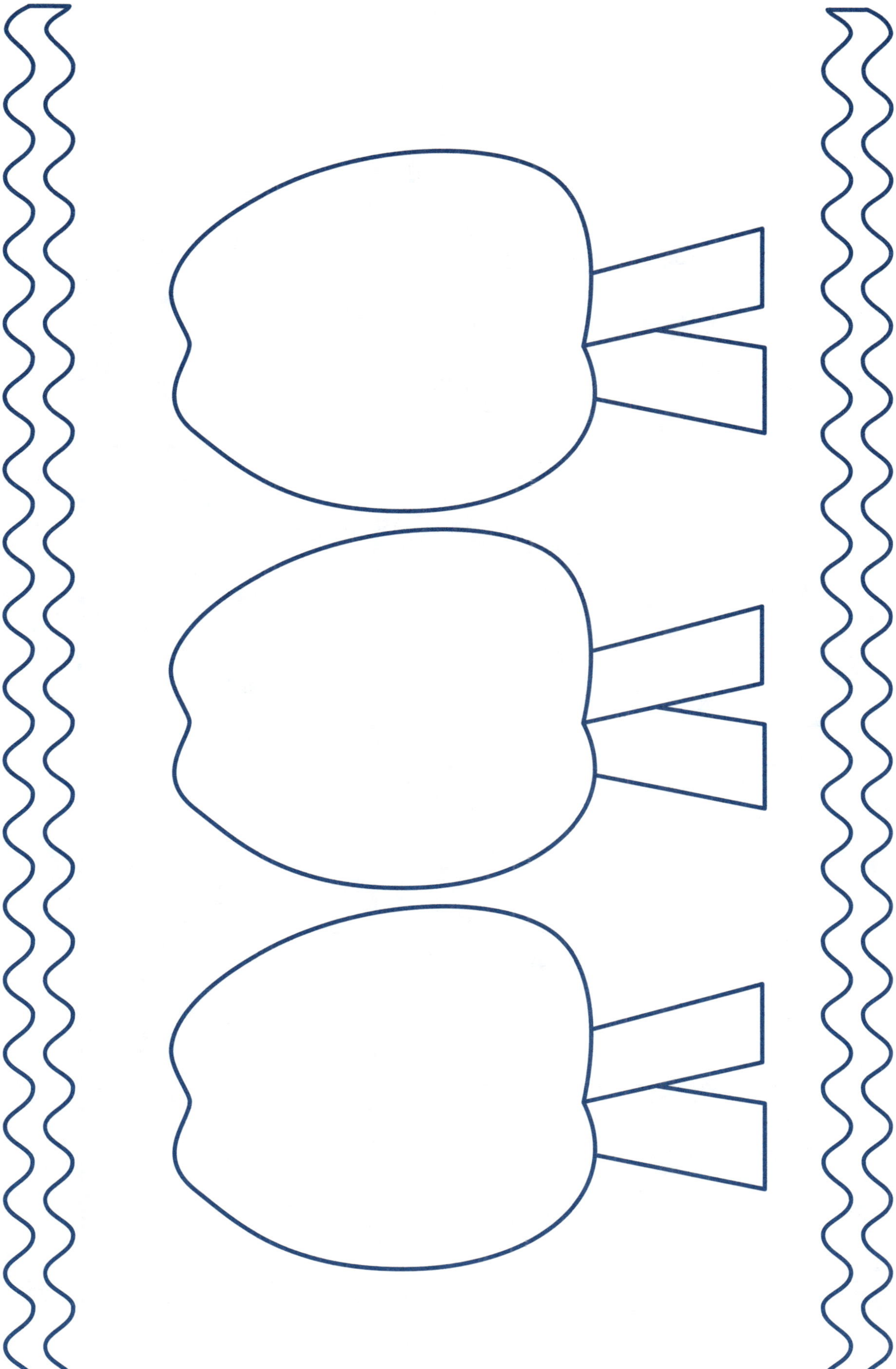

EXTRA! EXTRA!

Use striped and patterned ribbons, buttons, rickrack, or sequins to enhance this unique design.

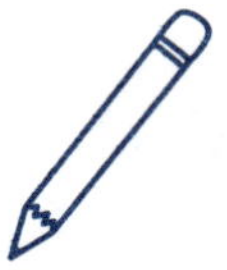

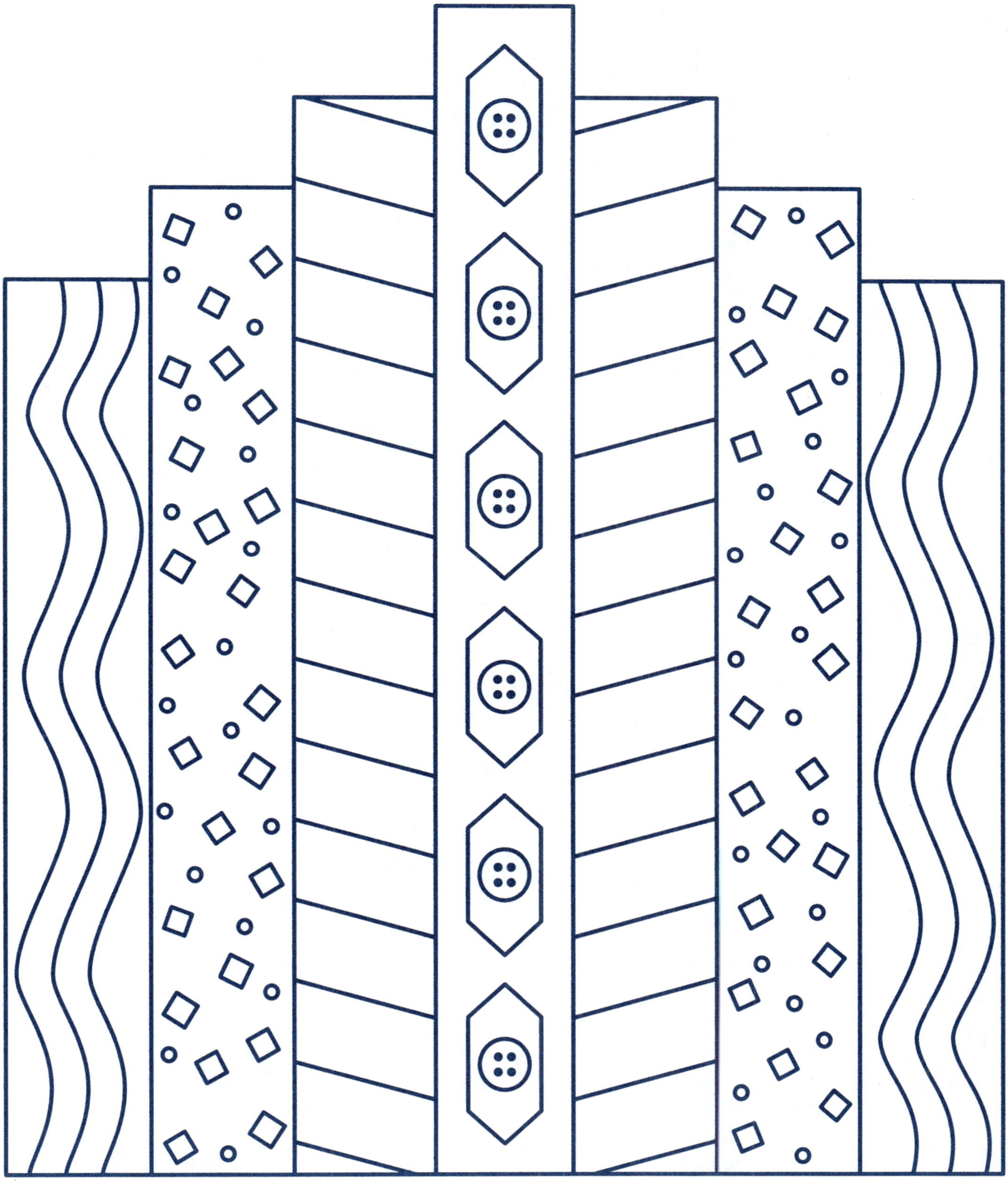

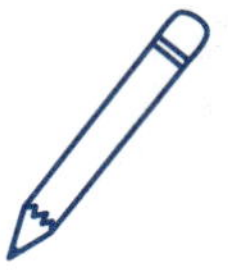

Test Transfer

Extra! Extra!

Make your own striped or patterned borders by using dimensional paint on solid-colored ribbons.

Test Transfer

Extra! Extra!

Replace each border with four different colors of ribbon.

Test Transfer

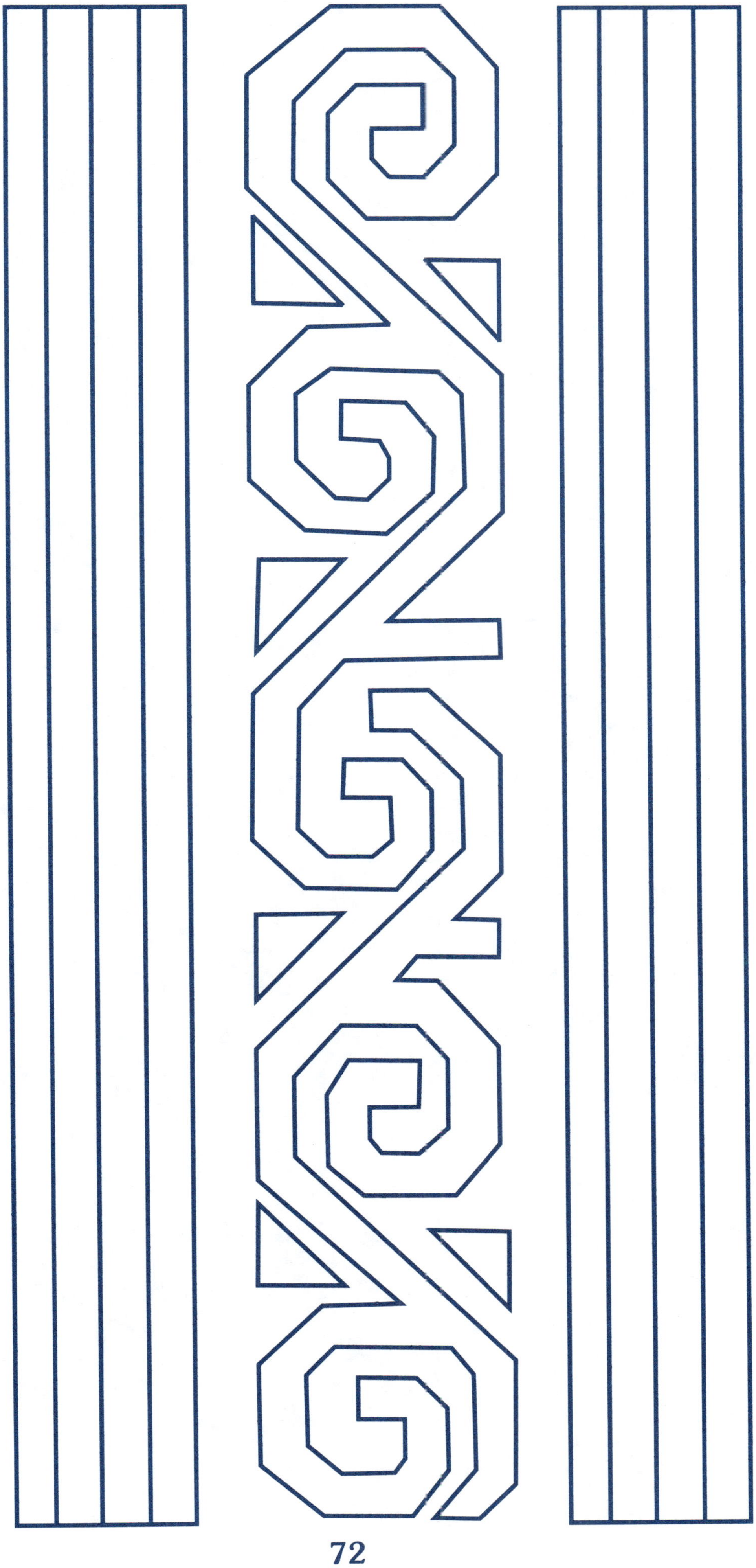

Extra! Extra!

Use silver metallic ribbon between the handle and the bristles of each paintbrush, outline with dimensional paint, and spatter paint the background for a truly artistic look. For an extra touch, replace paint strokes with ribbon.

Test Transfer

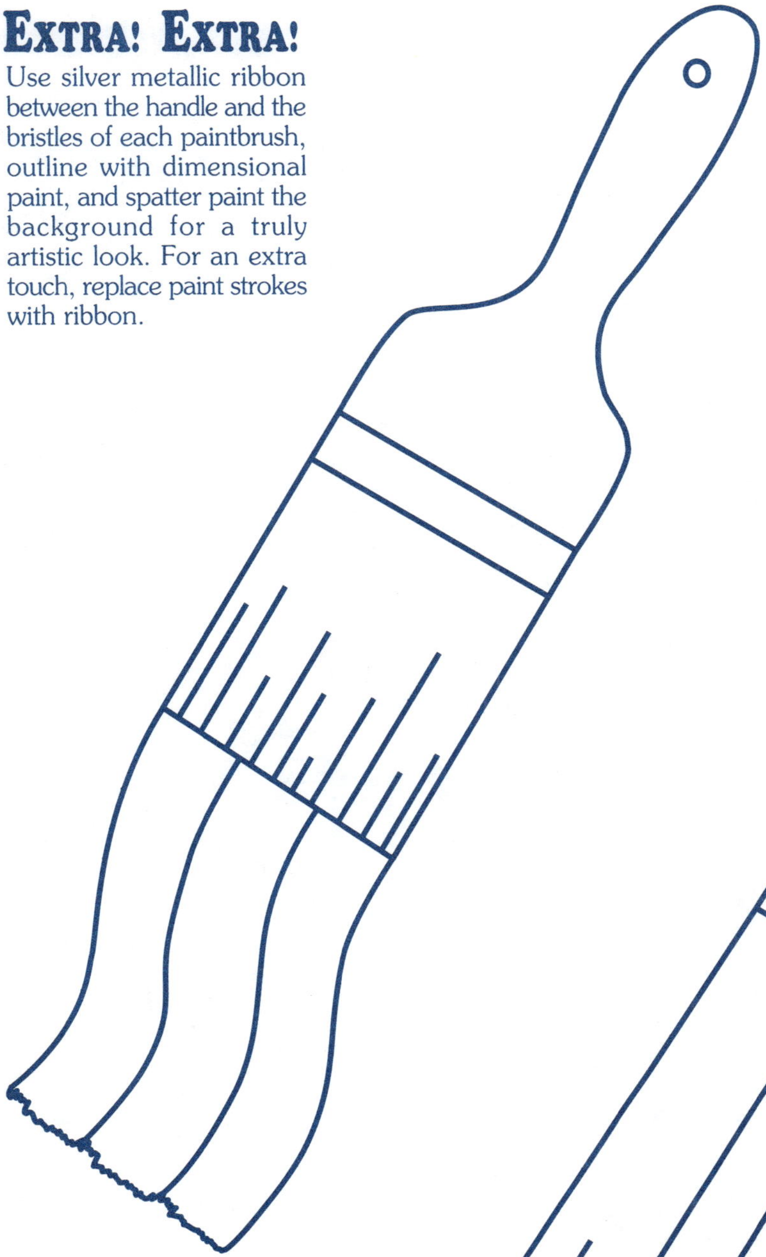

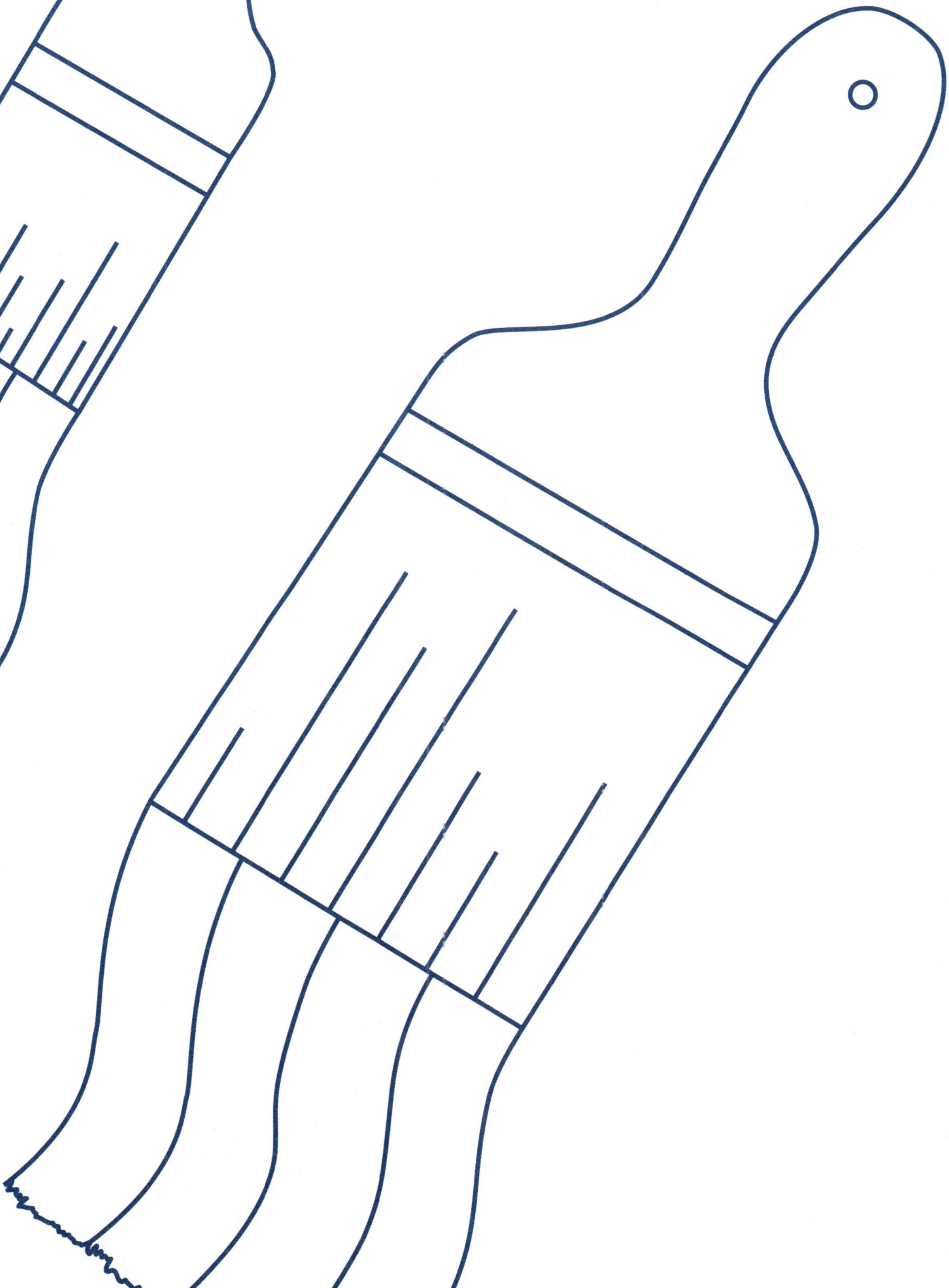

EXTRA! EXTRA!

Squeeze globs of bright dimensional paint onto the palette and add a touch of paint to the tip of the brush.

Test Transfer

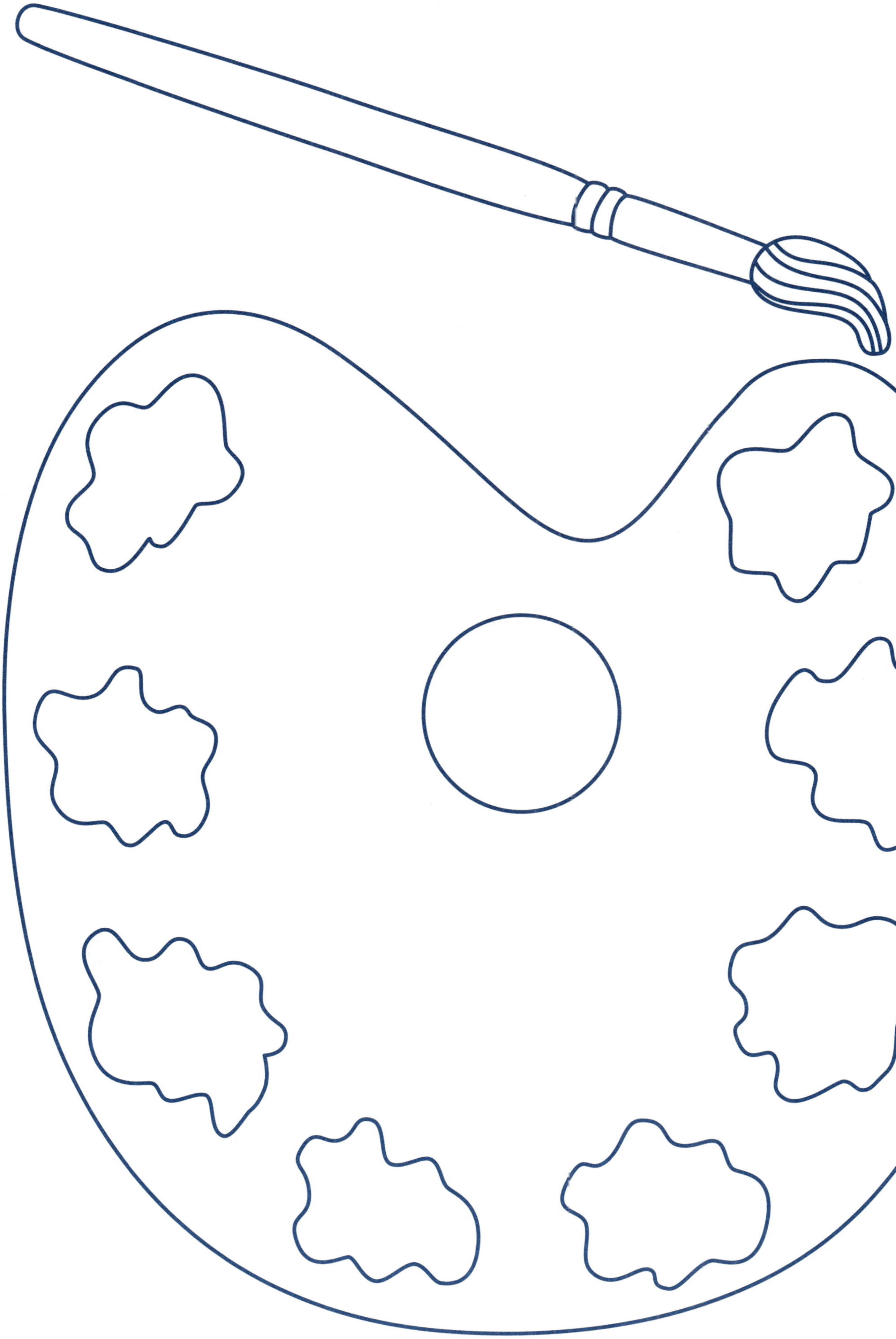

EXTRA! EXTRA!

Replace pinwheel center with a sequin or rhinestone and the handle with two lengths of rickrack twisted together.

Test Transfer

Extra! Extra!

Use dimensional paint stripes on the balls and rickrack for the grass. Dress up the mallets with lengths of ribbon.

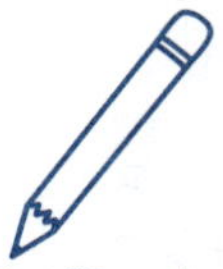

Test Transfer

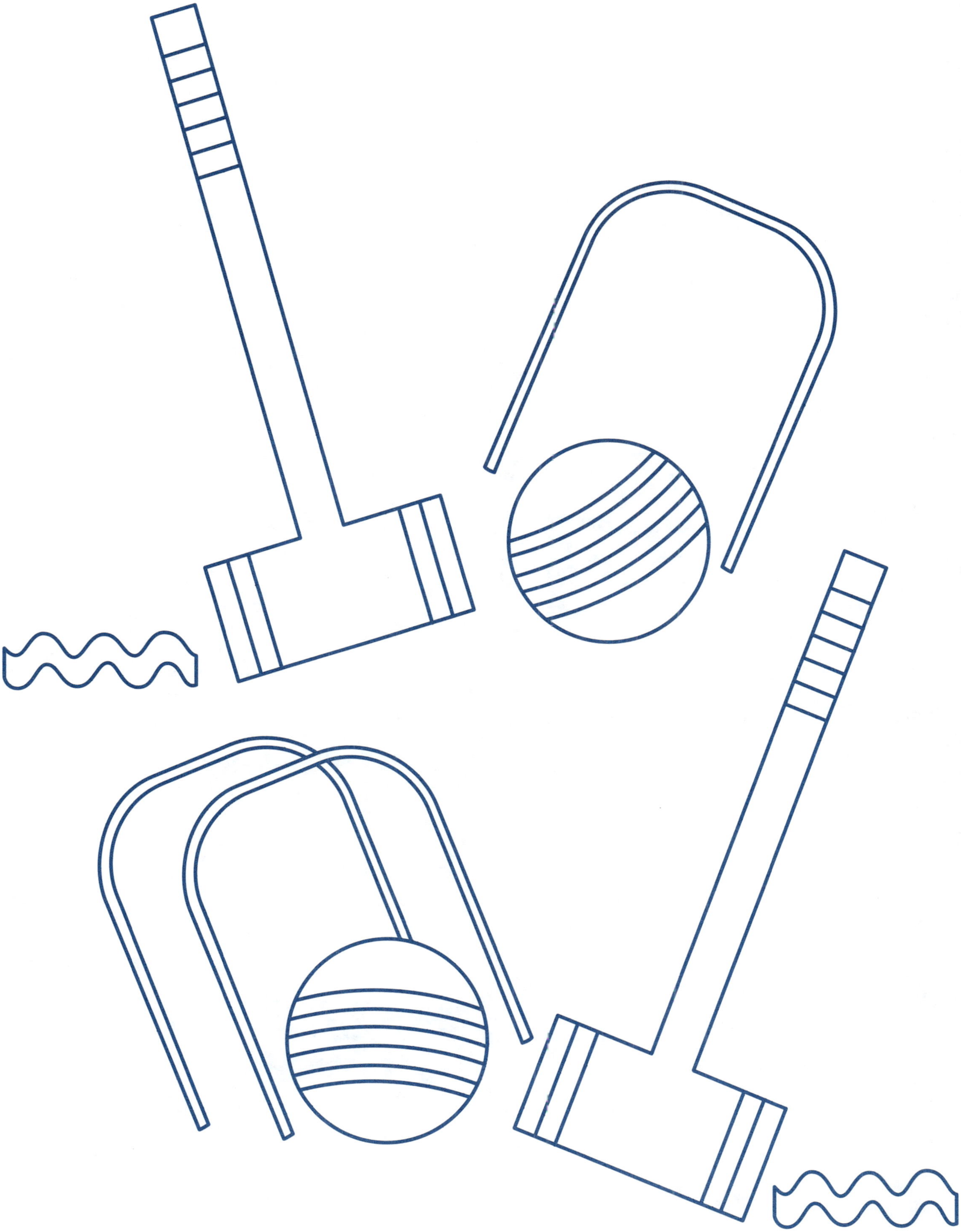

Extra! Extra!

Add dimension to your game with ribbons and cute buttons.

Test Transfer

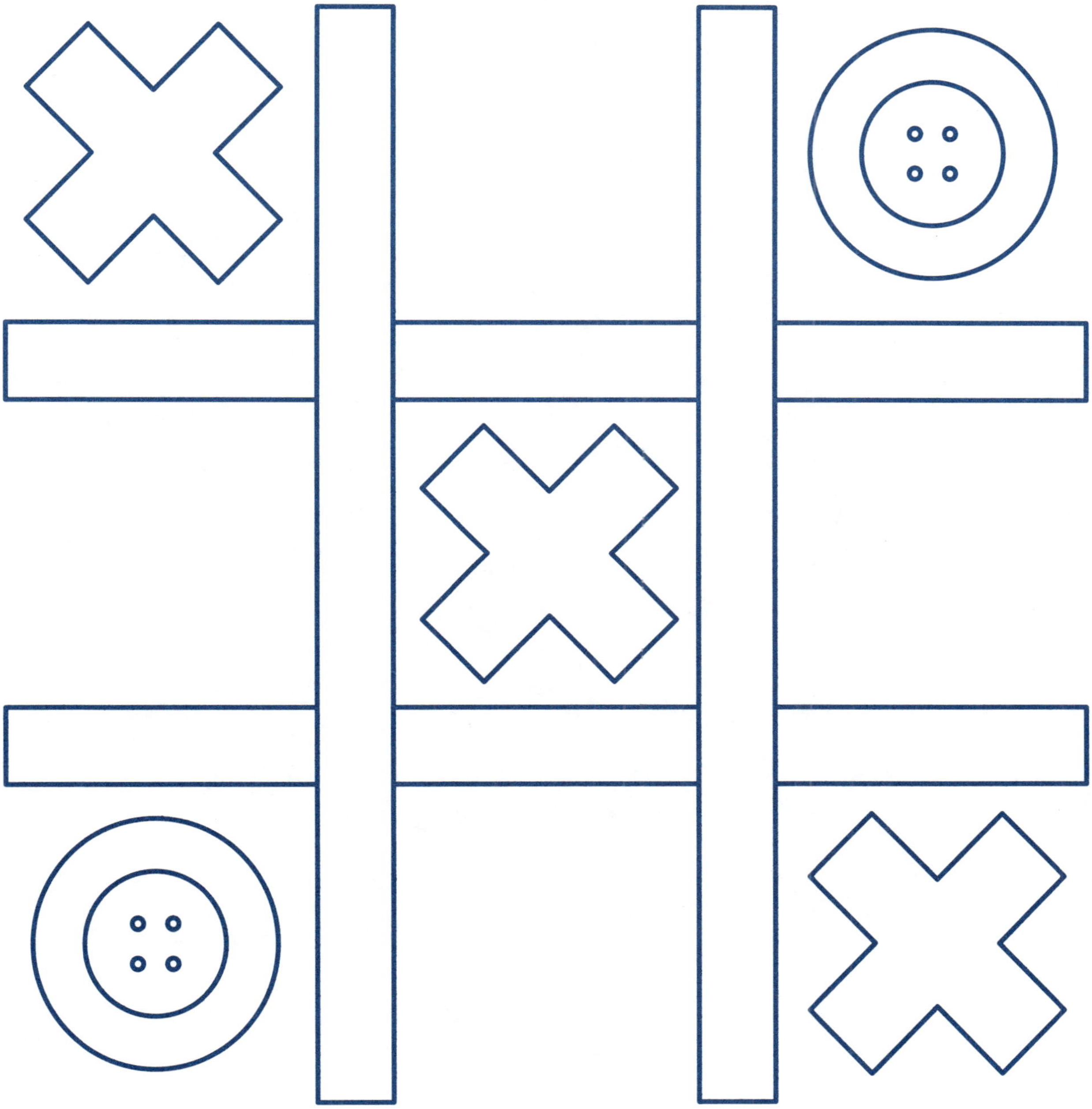

EXTRA! EXTRA!

Use buttons, jewels, and dimensional paint to decorate this top.

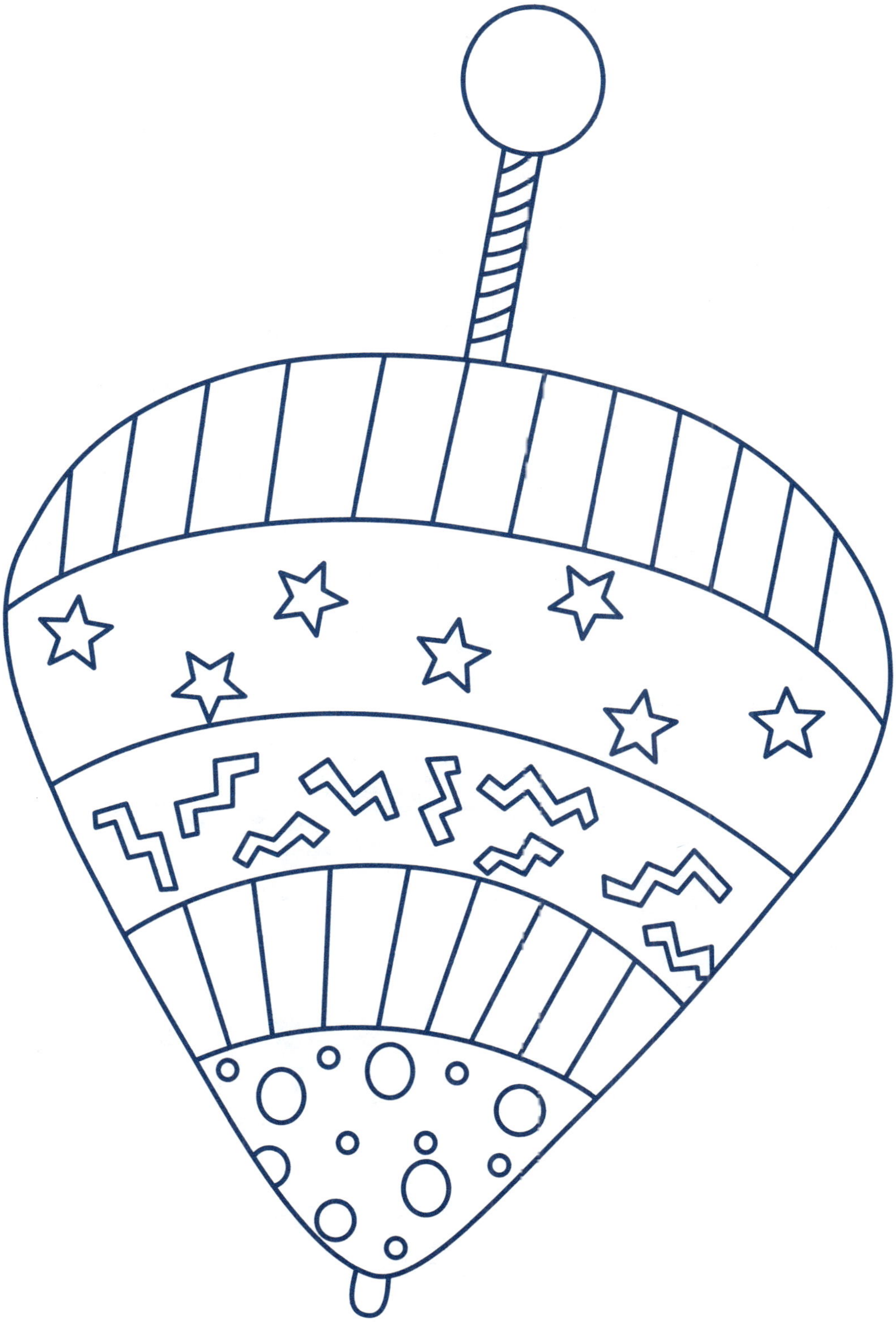

EXTRA! EXTRA!

Use real string and ribbon bows for the kite tail and ribbon stripes on the kite for a high-flying design.

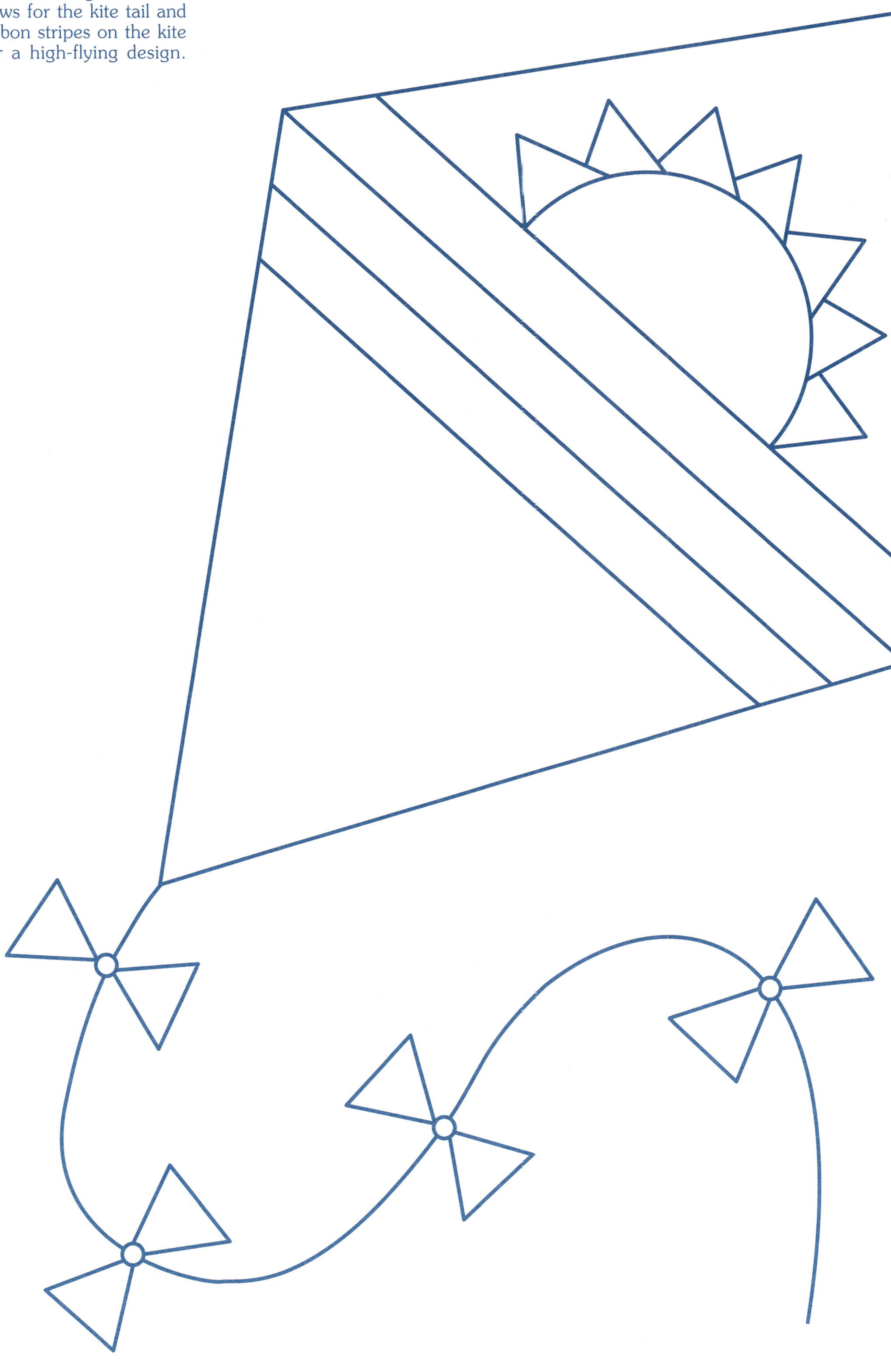

EXTRA! EXTRA!

Add ribbon stripes to the basket, a ribbon bow in the little girl's hair, and a large yellow button for the sun's center.

Extra! Extra!

Give this matey a fabric eye patch that can be lifted to reveal a button eye. Replace the stripes on his shirt with ribbon and add a ribbon border.

Test Transfer

Extra! Extra!

Use glitter paint, gold coin charms, or buttons for the coins in this treasure chest.

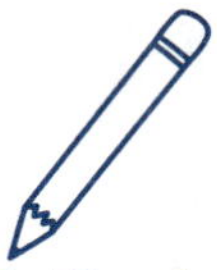

Extra! Extra!

Show team spirit by attaching ribbon stripes in your favorite team's colors to the helmet. Dimensional paint can be used for the football laces.

EXTRA! EXTRA!

Paint in your team colors and add dimensional paint outlines.

EXTRA! EXTRA!

Replace stars with buttons and add dimensional paint laces.

Test Transfer

EXTRA! EXTRA!

First spatter paint the Milky Way, then outline with glitter dimensional paint and add star studs for an out-of-this-world look.

Test Transfer

EXTRA! EXTRA!

Gussy up this cowpoke with a ribbon hatband, star button or charm for his badge, and dimensional paint designs on his boots. Use cording for his lasso.

Test Transfer

EXTRA! EXTRA!

Use folded ribbon lengths for this cool dude's hair.

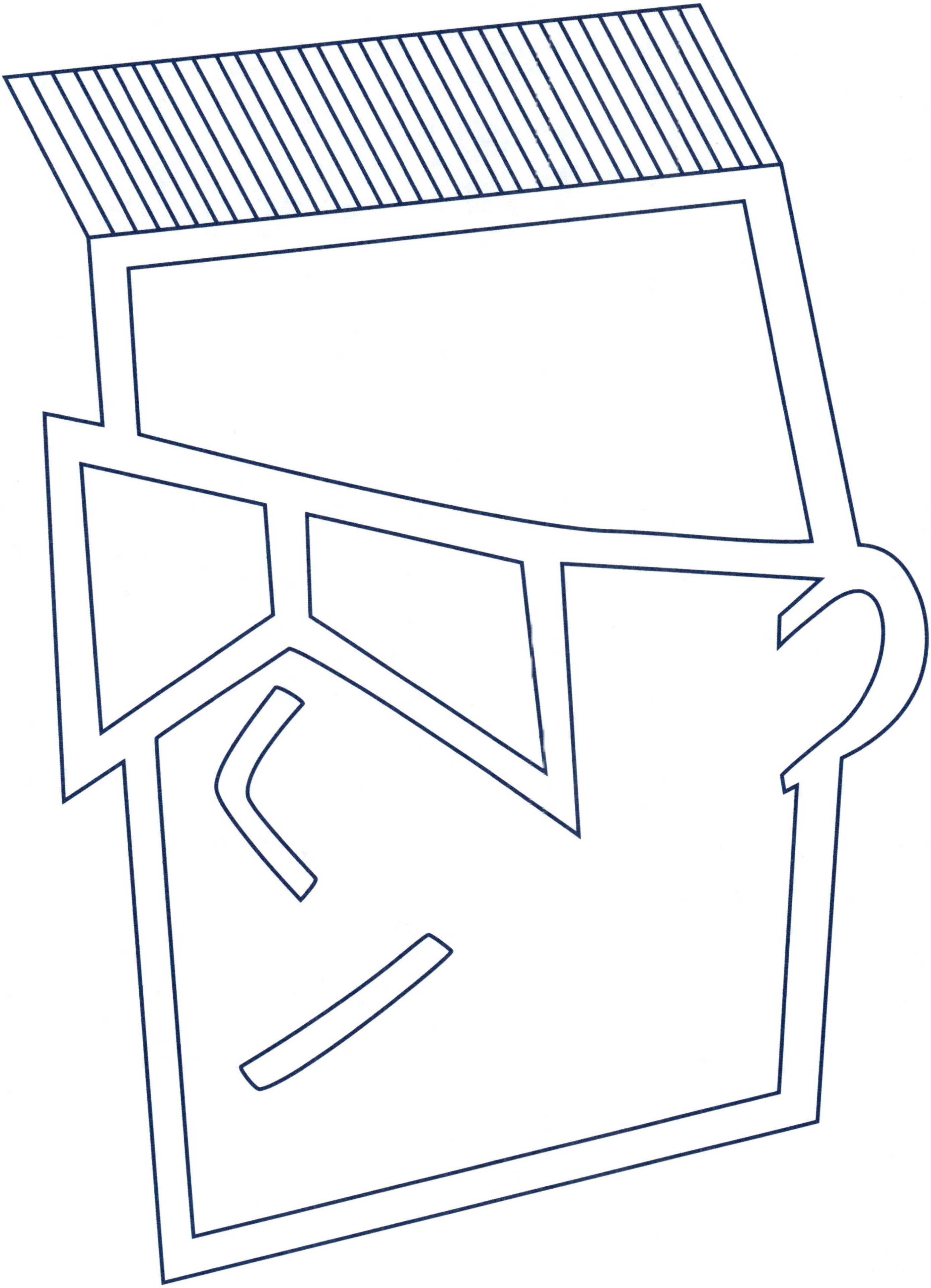

EXTRA! EXTRA!

Replace border with jumbo rickrack, then use dimensional paint and pom-poms spots to liven up this Jurassic creature.

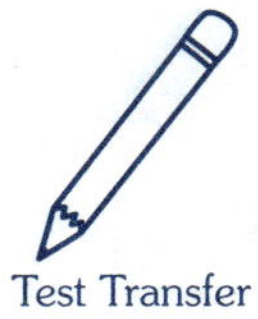
Test Transfer

EXTRA! EXTRA!

Use dimensional paint to outline, add rickrack grass, then accent with cute animal buttons to complete this barnyard scene.

Test Transfer

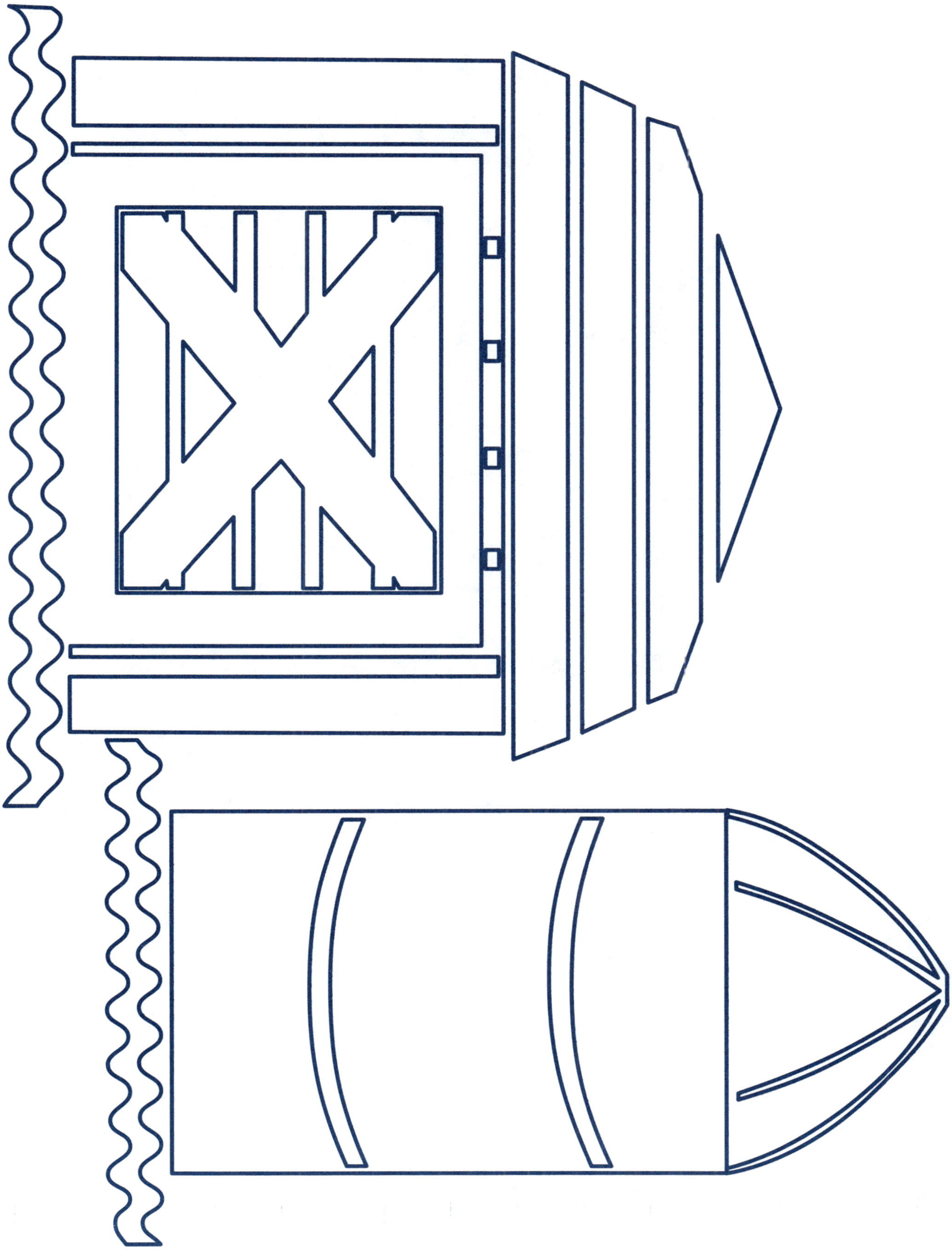

EXTRA! EXTRA!

Ring in the new school year by adding ribbon borders and a small bell to the school house.

Test Transfer

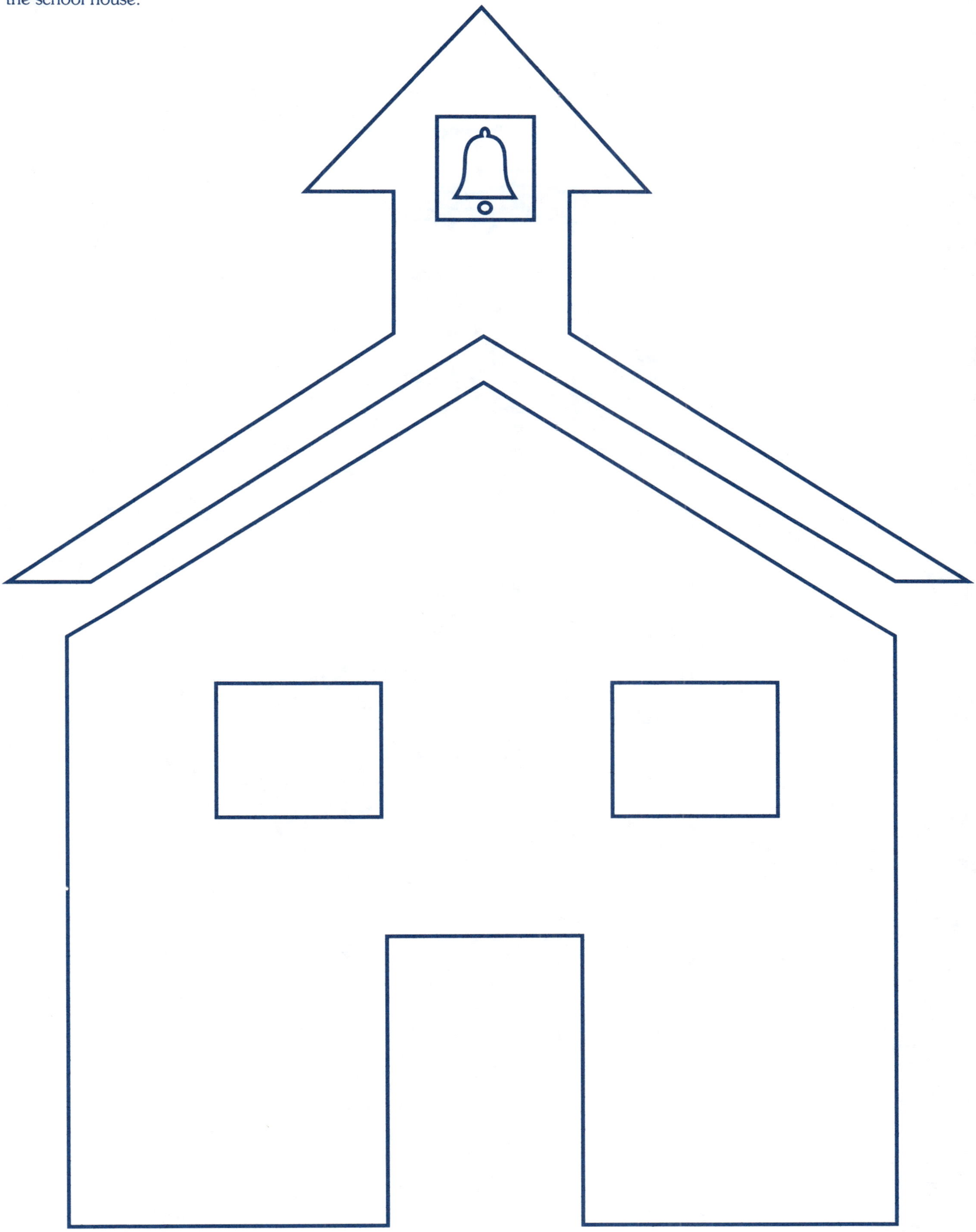

EXTRA! EXTRA!

Use glitter and dimensional paint to enhance the genie's bottle. Make the border into a magic carpet by adding a fringe of multi-colored ribbon lengths to the top and bottom edges.

EXTRA! EXTRA!

Decorate any of the next four horses with jewels, a button eye, and dimensional paint. Replace bridle with ribbon and add a ribbon bow to the tail.

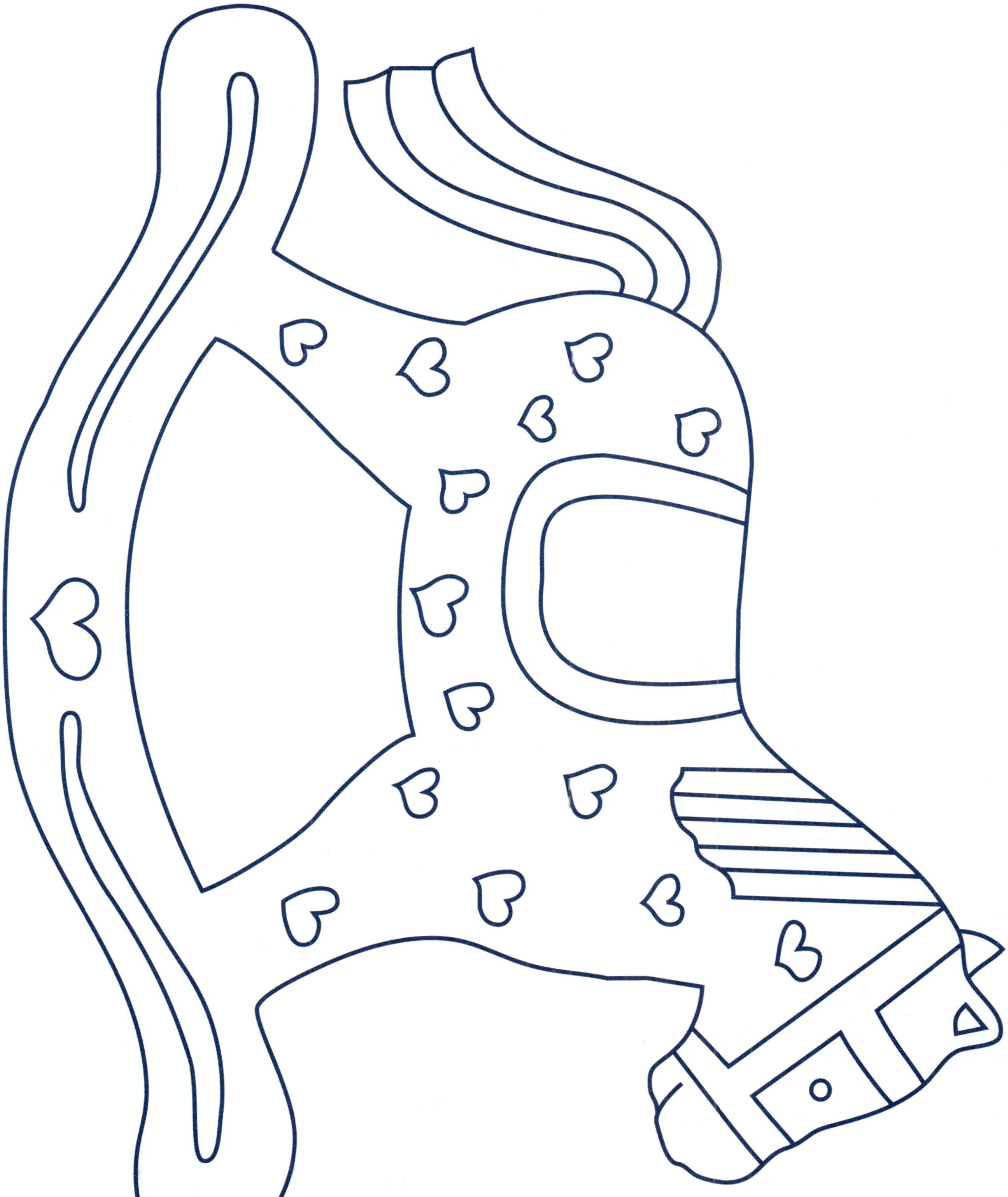

Test Transfer

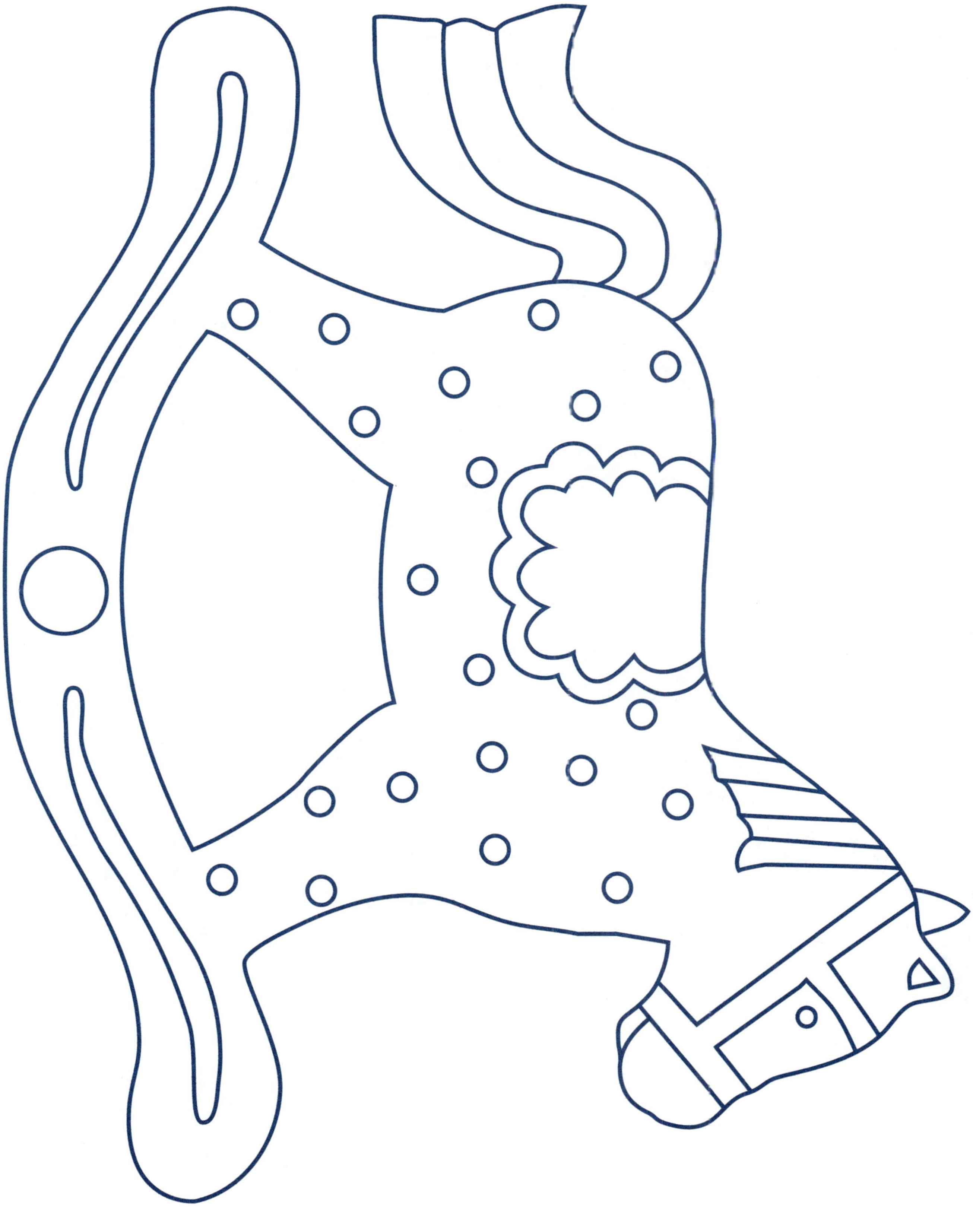

Test Transfer

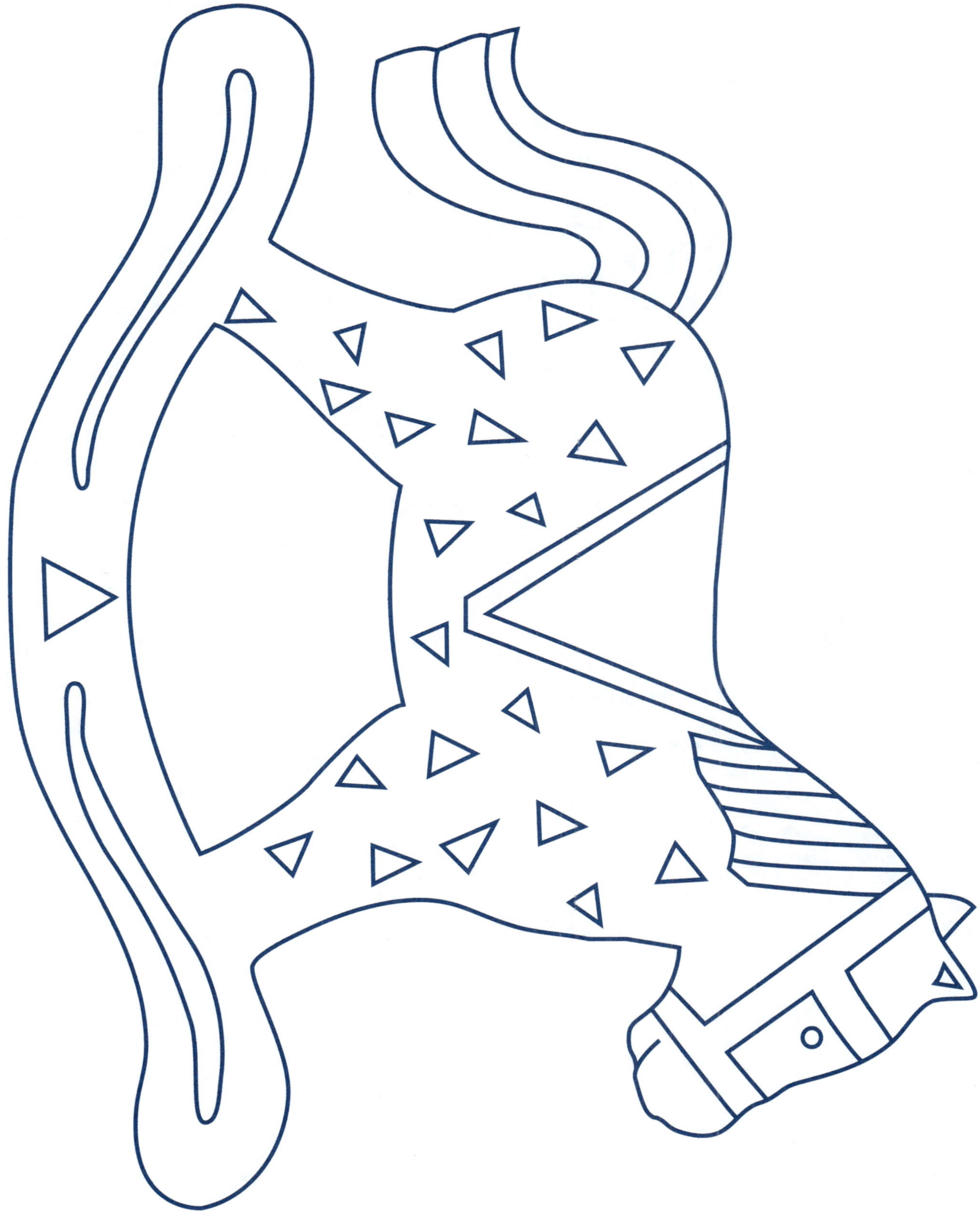

Test Transfer

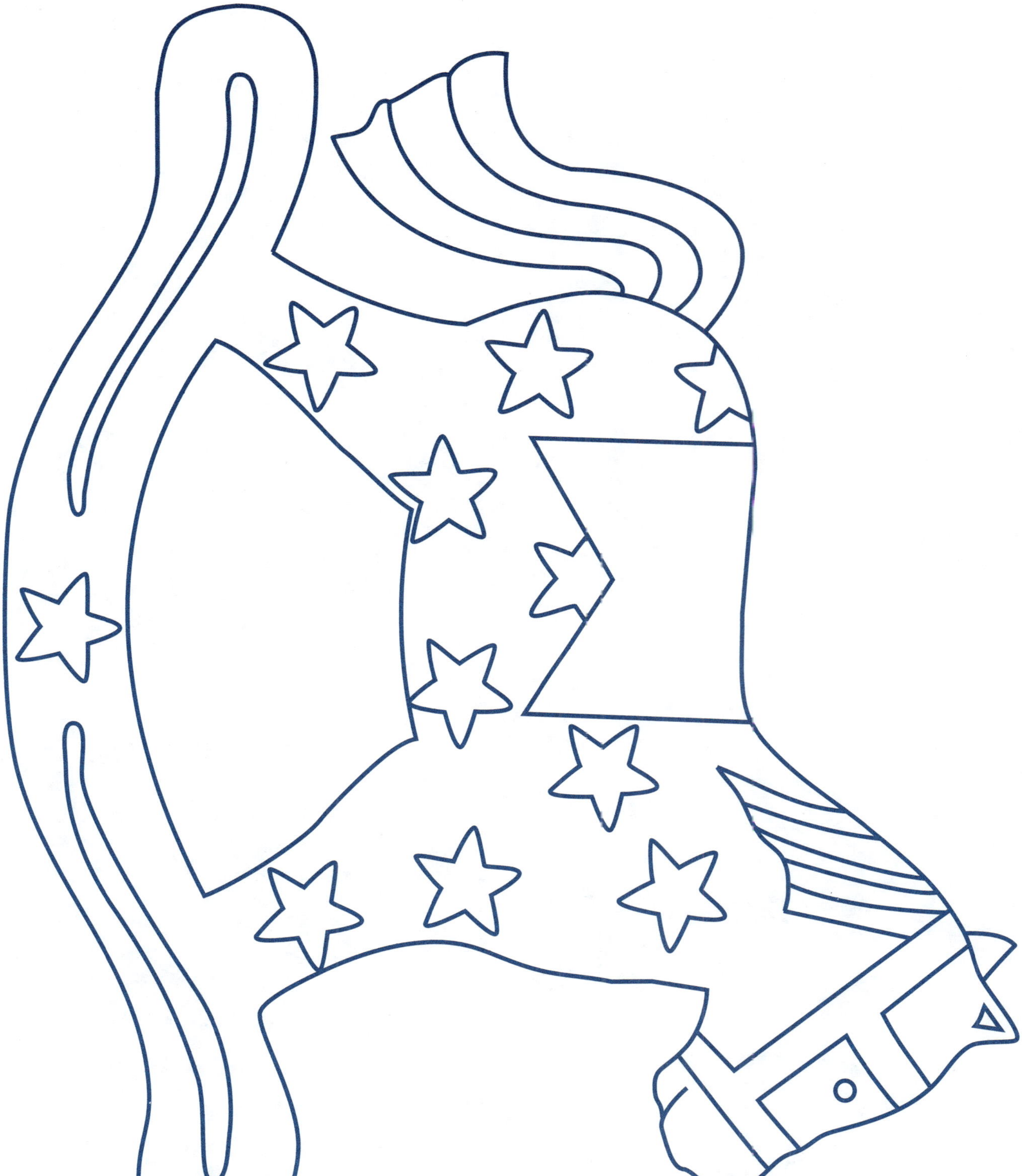

Extra! Extra!

Add narrow ribbon borders to form a block around each horse.

Test Transfer

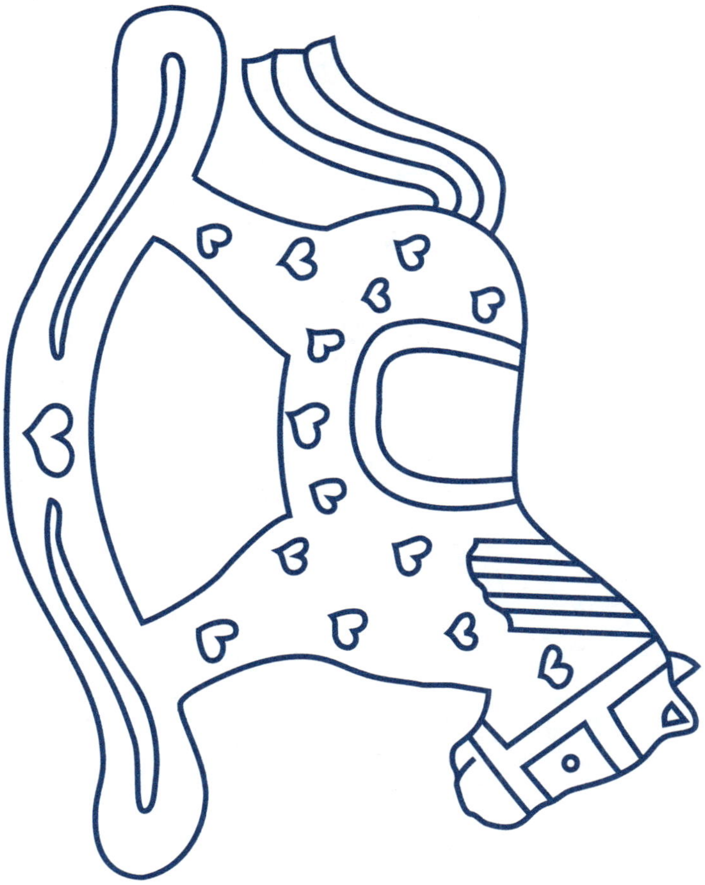

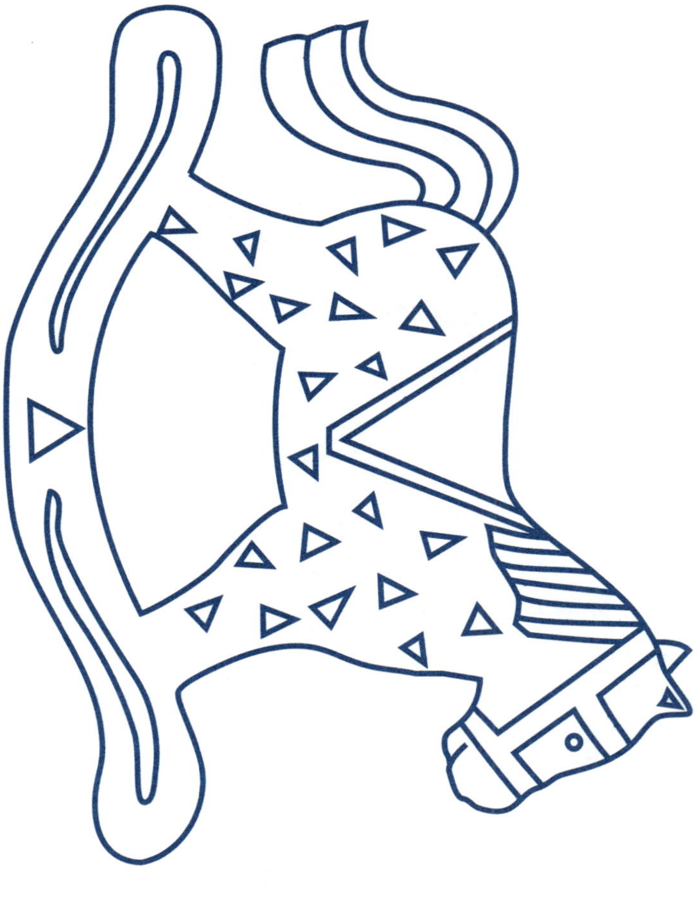

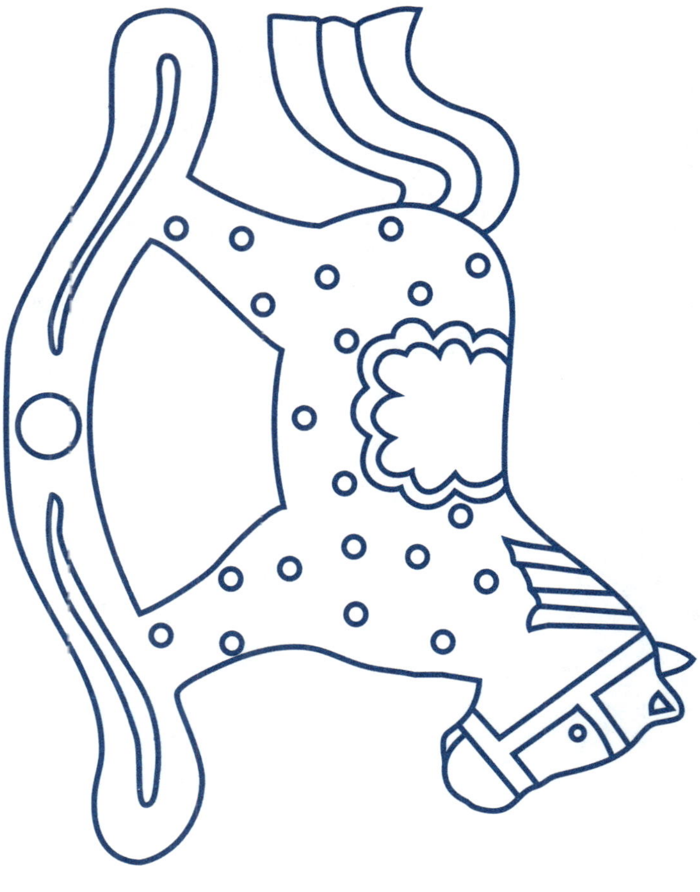

EXTRA! EXTRA!

Add ribbon bows on the toes and heart-shaped jewels to this adorable ballet design.

EXTRA! EXTRA!

Add spirit to the cheerleader's outfit by using paints and ribbons in your team's colors. Add ribbon bows to her shoes and pin a pom-pom made of ribbon lengths in her hand.

EXTRA! EXTRA!

Replace stripes with ribbon and add ribbon hair bows to this perky pyramid.

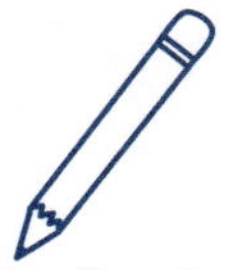

Test Transfer

EXTRA! EXTRA!

Add ribbon for stripes and hair bows, then place pom-poms or tassels in their hands.

Extra! Extra!

After transferring the design, sponge on blue paint for water. Paint the design, using dimensional and glitter paints for details. Add jewels for bubbles and rickrack for water. Complete the shirt by adding rickrack around the sleeves and hem.

Test Transfer

Test Transfer

EXTRA! EXTRA!

Sprinkle very fine iridescent glitter on wet paint and replace border by gluing braid or cording in its place.

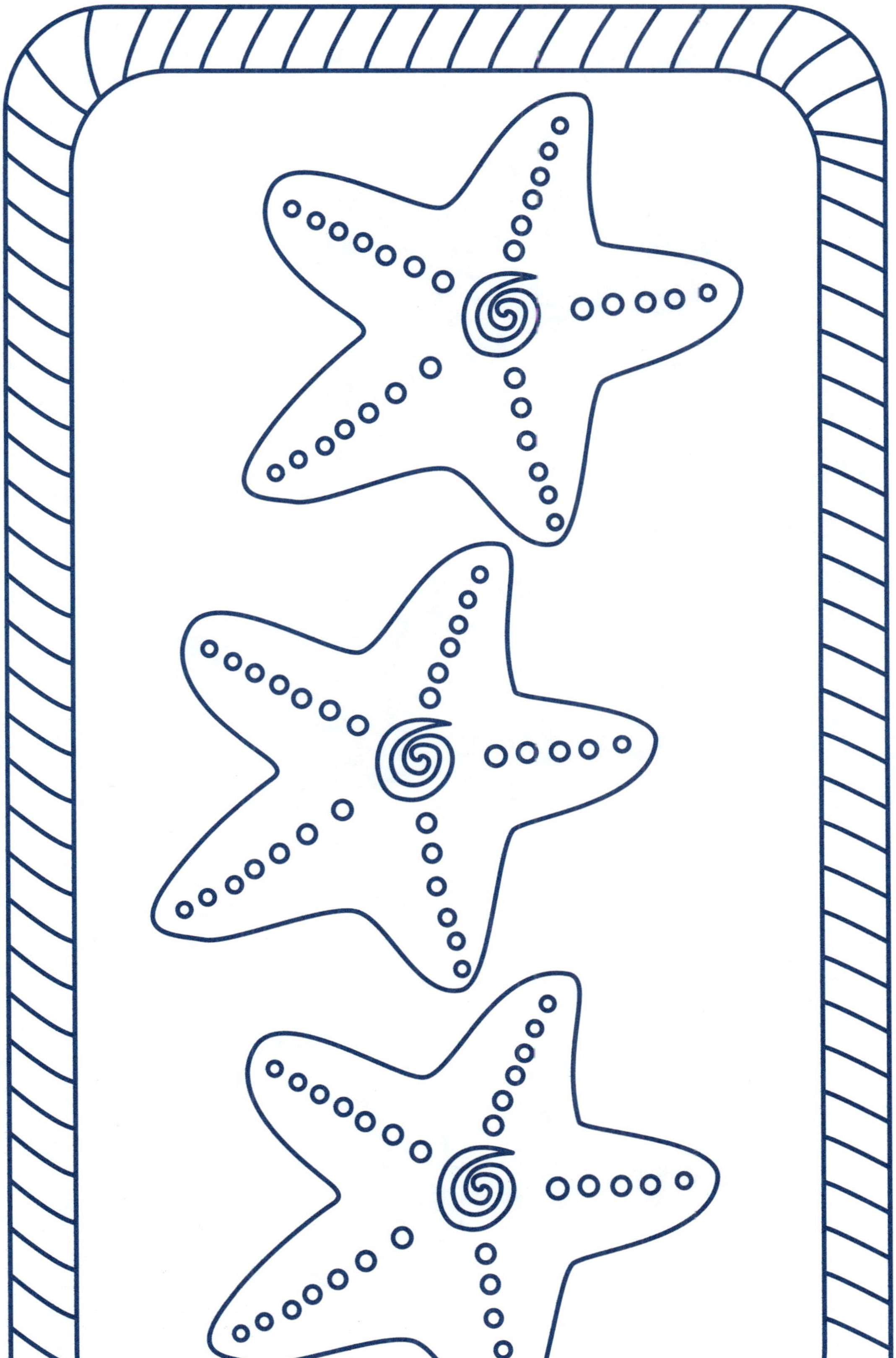

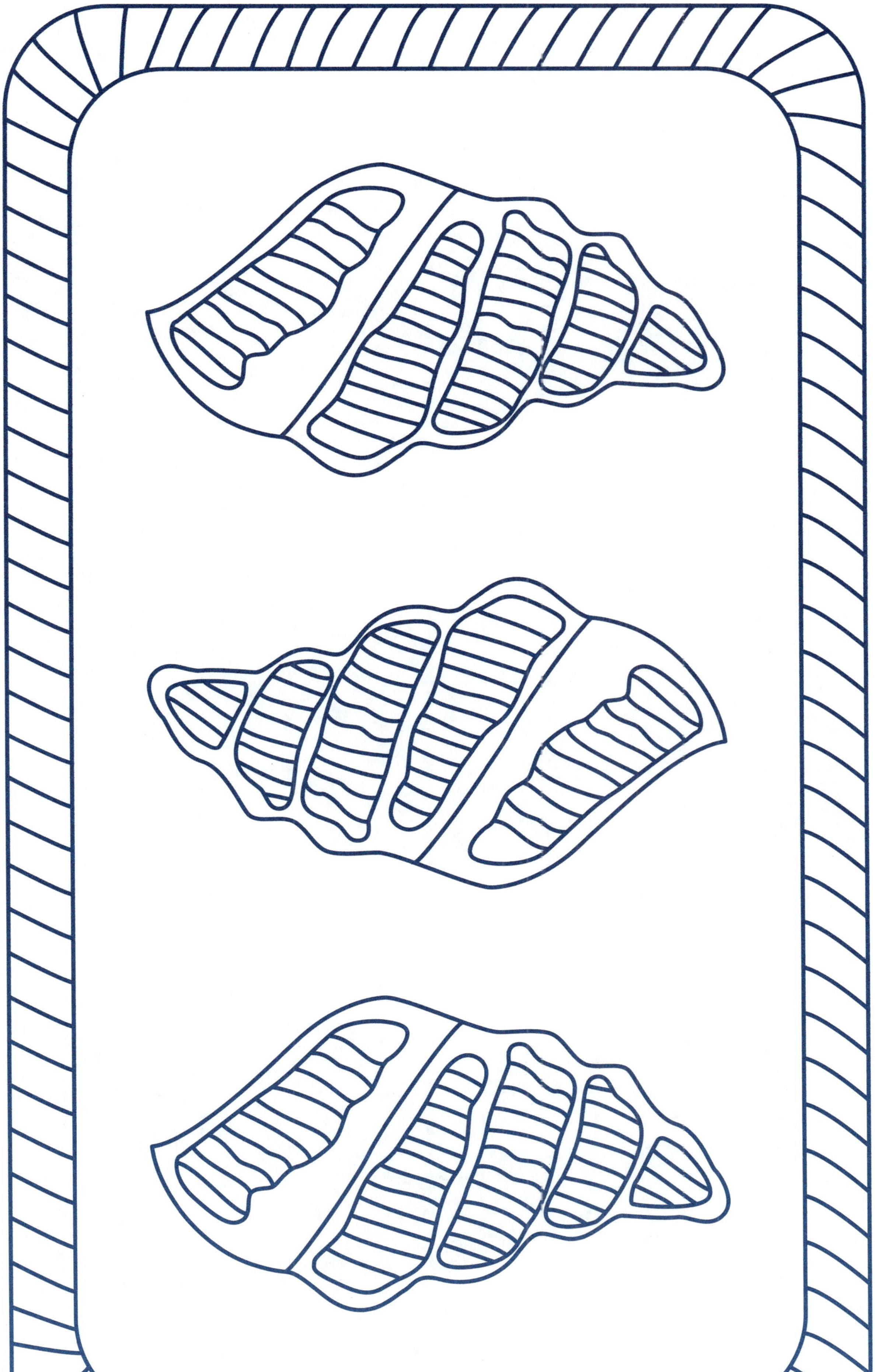

Test Transfer

EXTRA! EXTRA!

For a smaller garment, trim one of the fish from the design. Use jewels for the bubbles, dotted ribbon for the stripes, and finish by adding a bow at the top of each fish.

Extra! Extra!

Use rickrack for waves, jewels or pearls for bubbles, and glitter paint on the fish and seashells.

Test Transfer

EXTRA! EXTRA!

Button or charm stars, ribbon flags, shiny dimensional paint windows, and glitter accents bring this fairy-tale castle to life.

Test Transfer

Extra! Extra!

Paint this fish and water with glitter paint; add curly ribbon or rickrack for seaweed.

Test Transfer

EXTRA! EXTRA!

A spray of glitter paint and blue jumbo rickrack waves certainly add to this whale of a design.

Extra! Extra!

Add buttons for eyes and jumbo rickrack borders as a frame for this leggy guy.

Test Transfer

EXTRA! EXTRA!

A pretty ribbon border turns this slow but sure snail into a winner.

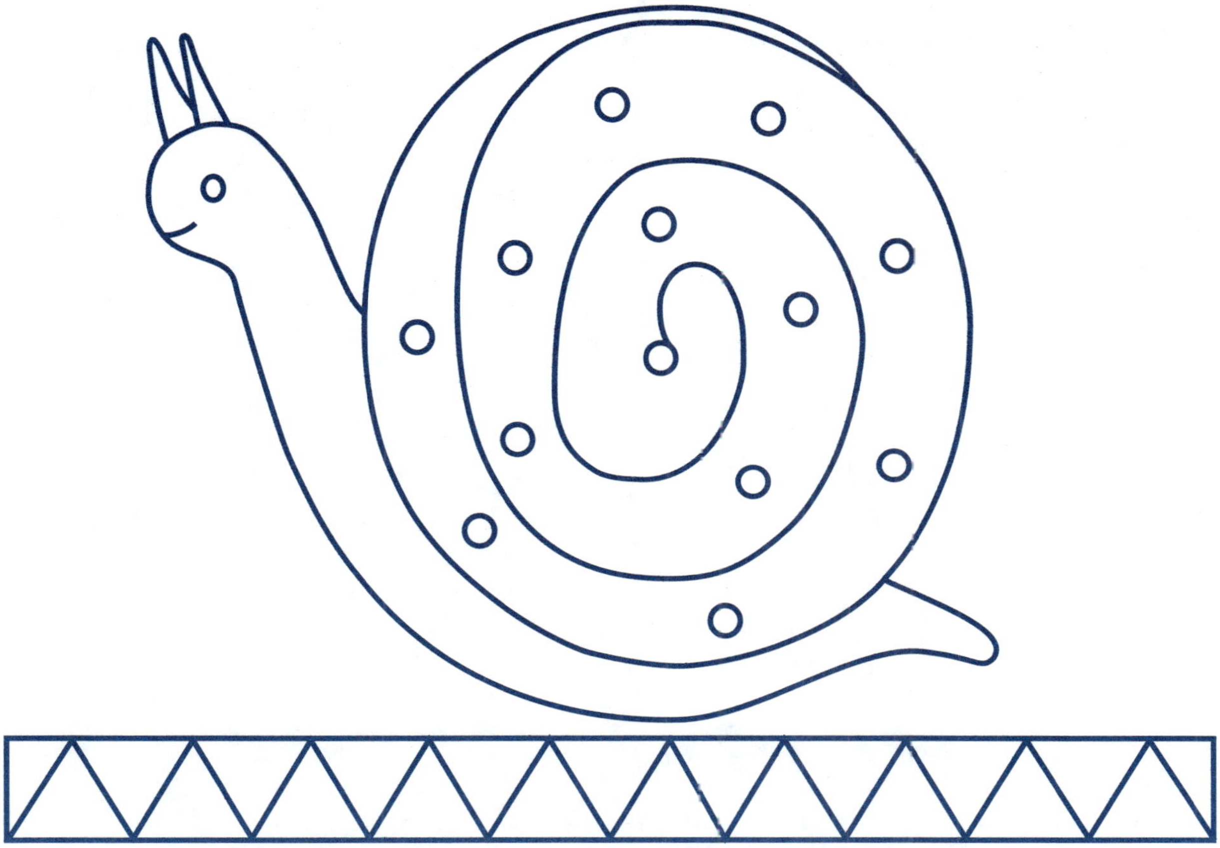

EXTRA! EXTRA!

Replace waves with blue rickrack, then add dimensional paint spots and buttons for eyes.

Extra! Extra!

Add one or both of these little frogs to pant legs or a skirt to coordinate with your frog shirt.

Test Transfer

EXTRA! EXTRA!

Use rickrack for the waves, buttons for eyes, and dimensional paint for the beaks and feet of these cute feathered friends.

Extra! Extra!

Replace stripes on this turtle with jumbo rickrack and use a button for his eye.

Test Transfer

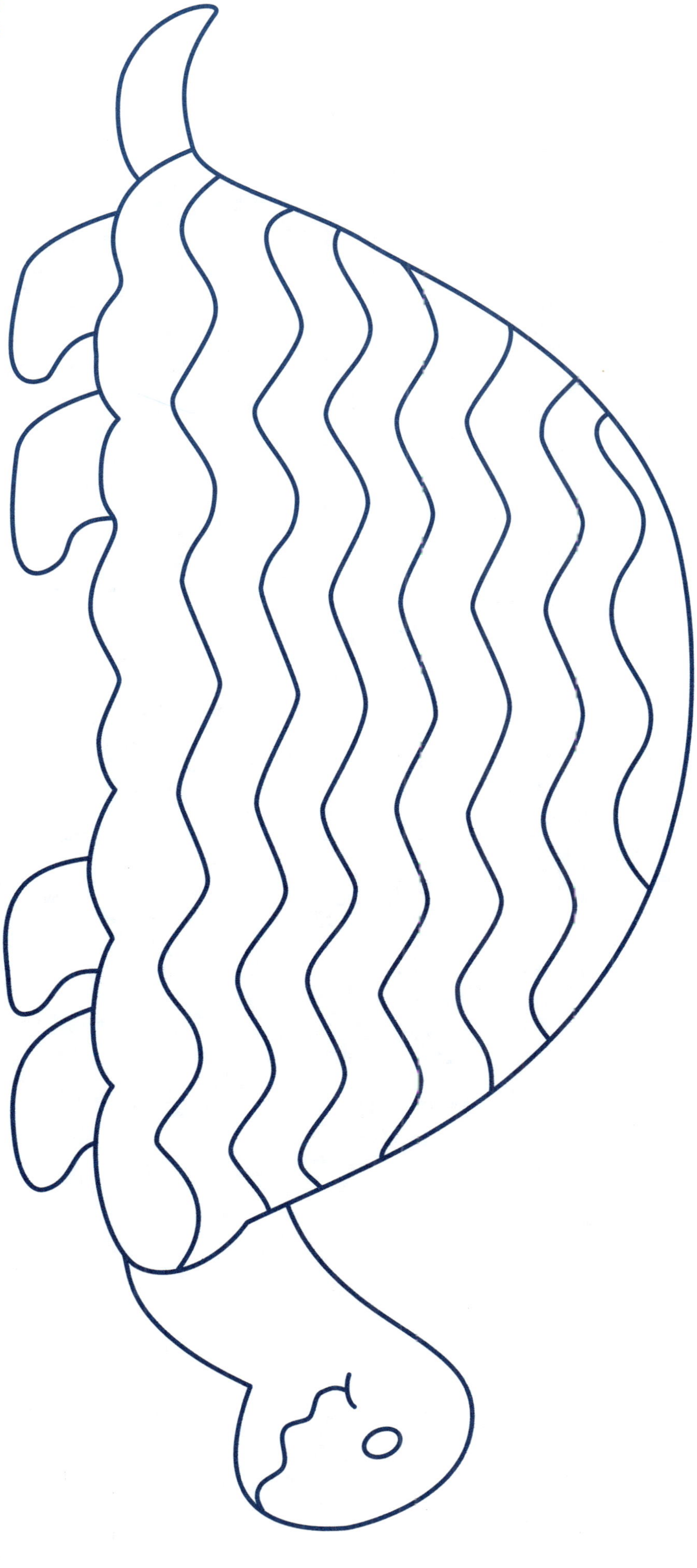

Extra! Extra!

Use glitter paint to outline the turtles' spots and then replace waves with rickrack to make this a delightful shirt for your little one.

EXTRA! EXTRA!

Replace the segments of this snake with different-colored ribbons.

Test Transfer

Extra! Extra!

Use dimensional paint, a rickrack border, and buttons to liven up this cute lizard.

Test Transfer

Extra! Extra!

Use red polka-dot ribbon for these ladybug bodies, then outline with dimensional paint. Add buttons to their antennas and some rickrack to the sleeves and bottom of your shirt for a coordinating touch.

Test Transfer

Extra! Extra!

Use patterned ribbons for the bumblebee body, then outline in dimensional paint. Sew on some flower buttons and make easy-to-remove daisies by gluing two ribbon lengths for leaves and a pin back to each silk flower bloom.

Test Transfer

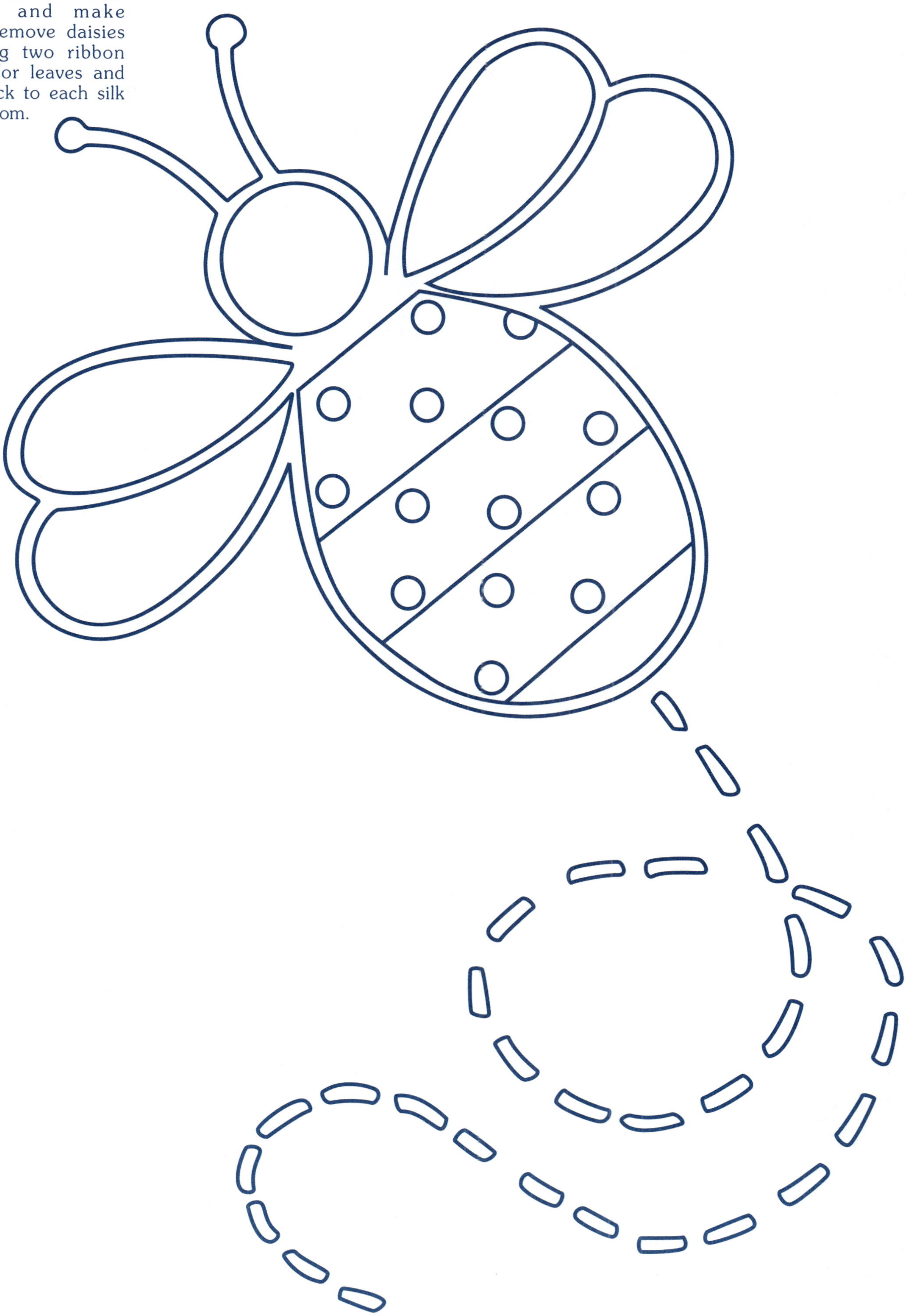

Test Transfer

EXTRA! EXTRA!

Make this design really buzz by adding a cute ribbon border and pinning on bee wings tied from organza ribbon.

EXTRA! EXTRA!

Embellish this cute mouse with a button or wiggle eye, a pom-pom nose, ribbon whiskers, and a bow on her tail.

EXTRA! EXTRA!

Replace the stripes on this cat with colorful ribbons and you'll be the cat's meow!

EXTRA! EXTRA!

Outline this pooch in dimensional paint, then add buttons for eyes and some pom-poms to his neckerchief.

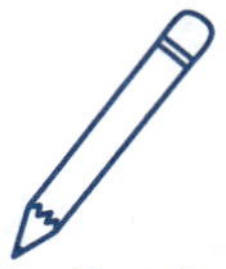

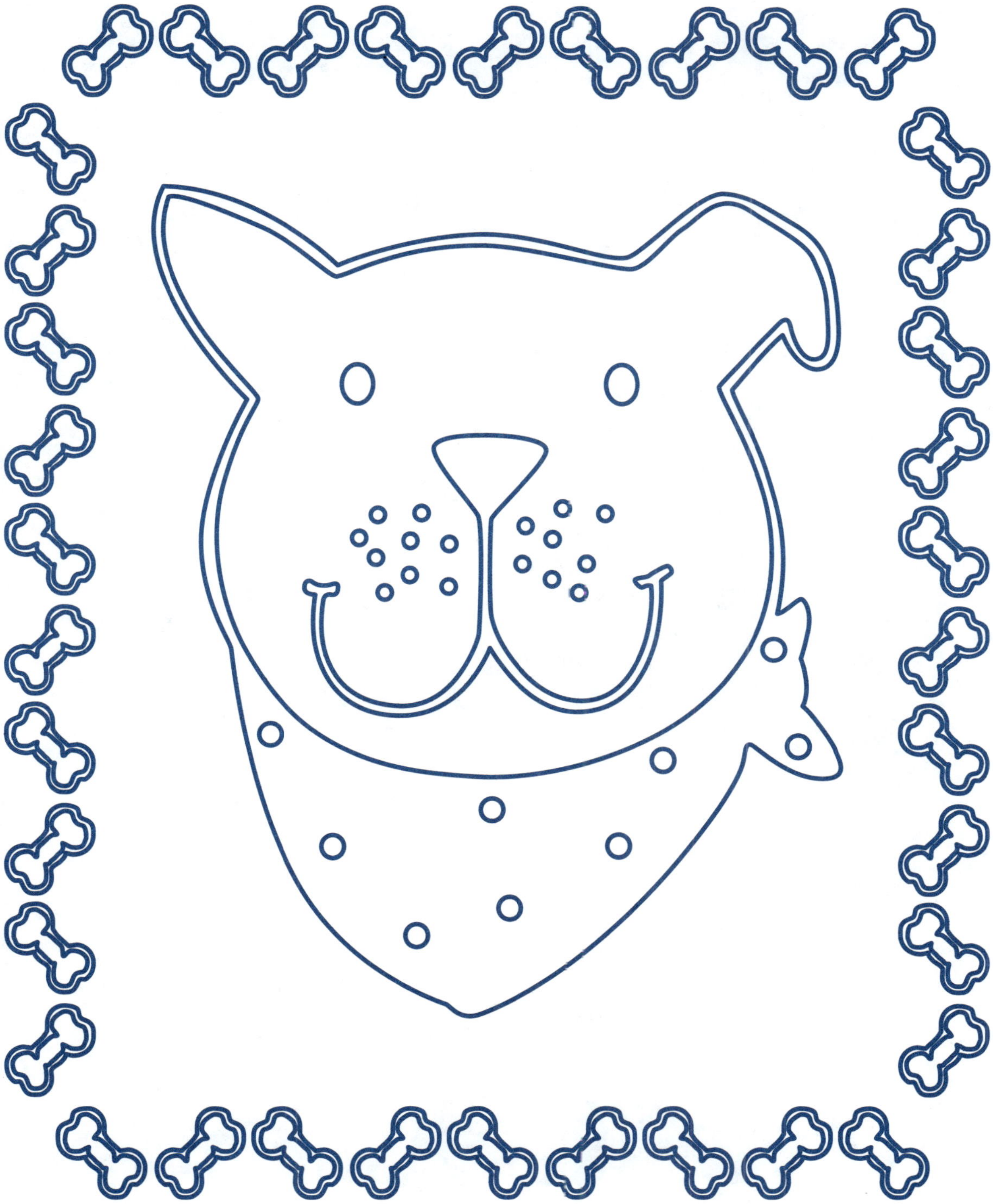

Test Transfer

Extra! Extra!

Use buttons for eyes, dimensional paint for spots, and replace grass with rickrack.

Extra! Extra!

Replace the faces of the bunnies with fabric-covered buttons and draw the bunnies' facial features with permanent pen. Use pom-poms for tails, rickrack for grass, and dimensional paint for carrot leaves.

EXTRA! EXTRA!

Use dimensional paint for the carrots, the bunny's face, and a scattering of dots. Finish by adding a pom-pom tail and a festive bow.

Test Transfer

EXTRA! EXTRA!

Attach a small jingle bell to each lamb's neck.

Test Transfer

Extra! Extra!

Add a button nose, a curly ribbon tail, and a ribbon bow to this little piggy.

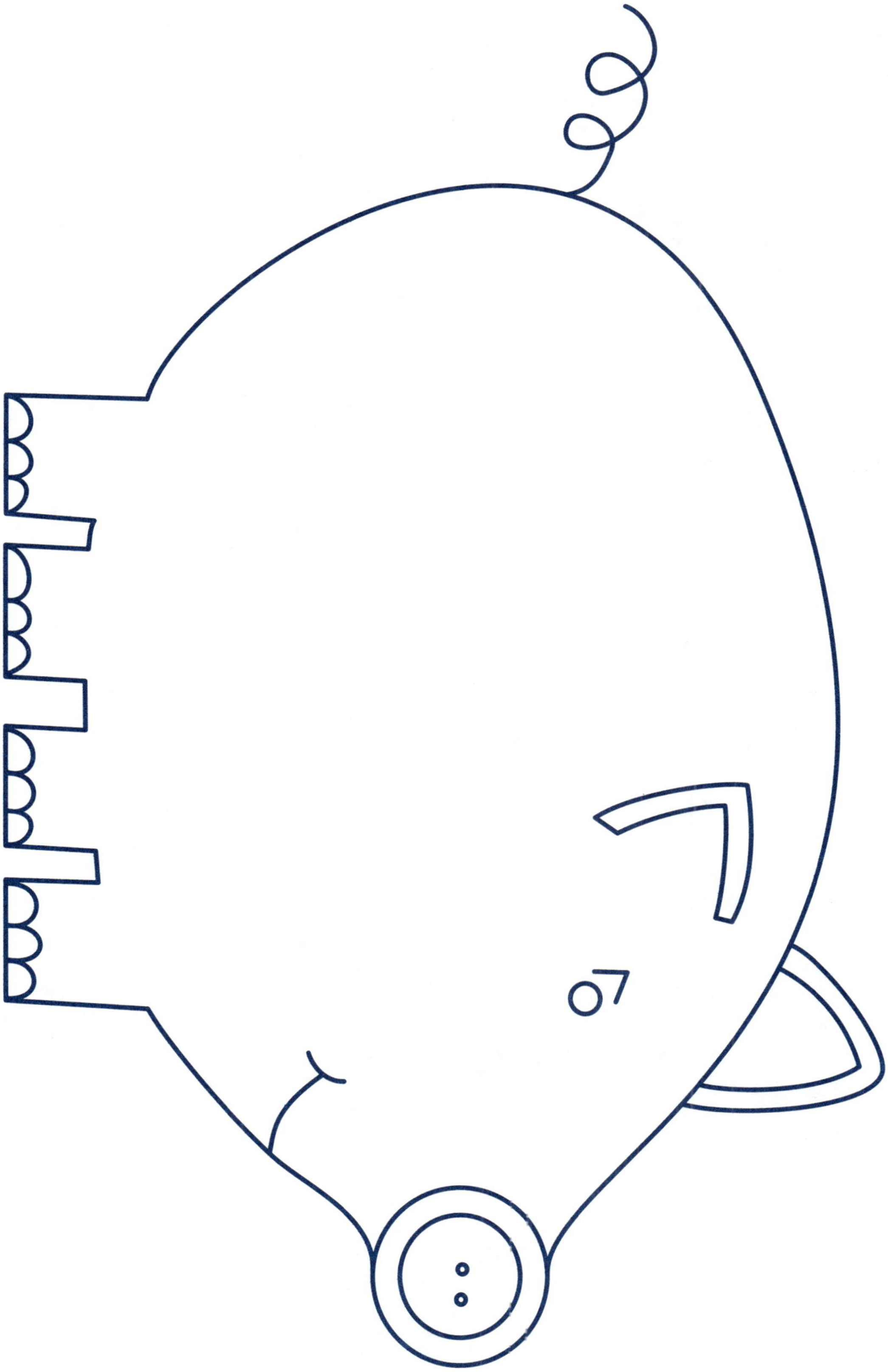

Extra! Extra!

Add a ribbon border, buttons for eyes, a ribbon bow, and a bell to this checkerboard cow.

Test Transfer

EXTRA! EXTRA!

Add dimensional paint details and use a patterned ribbon to replace the roof and post.

Test Transfer

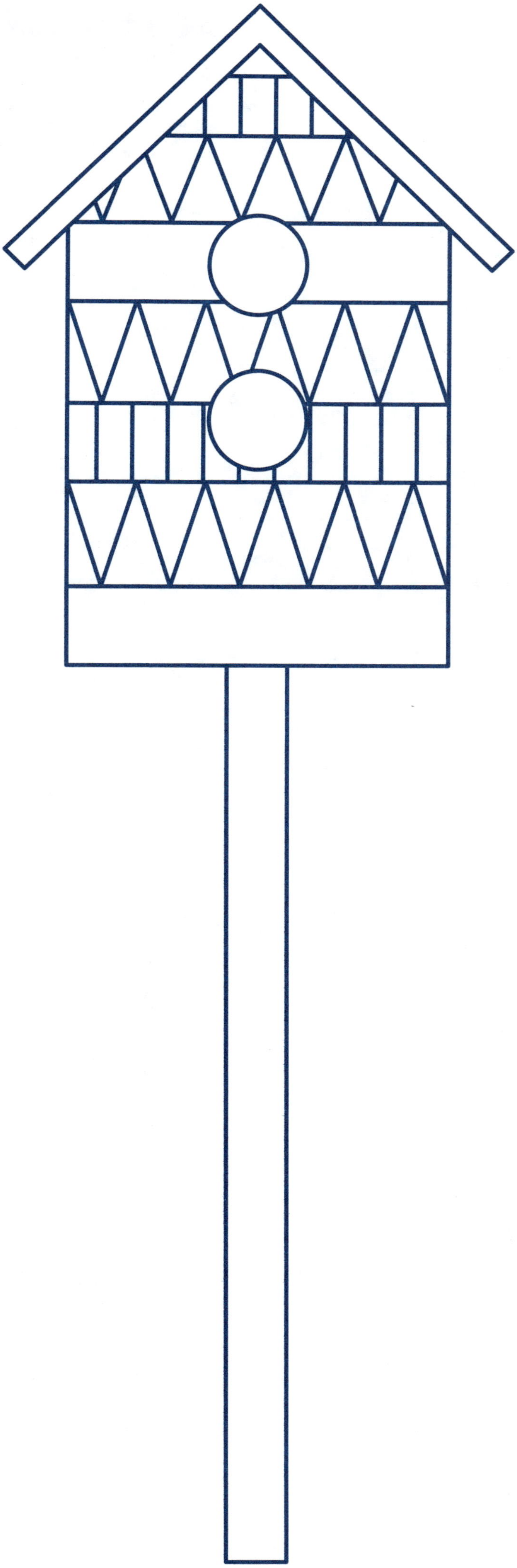

EXTRA! EXTRA!

Outline this playful character with thick lines of dimensional paint and add buttons for eyes.

Test Transfer

Extra! Extra!

Dress up this elephant by adding a ribbon border and flag, star jewels, and by outlining with dimensional paint.

Test Transfer

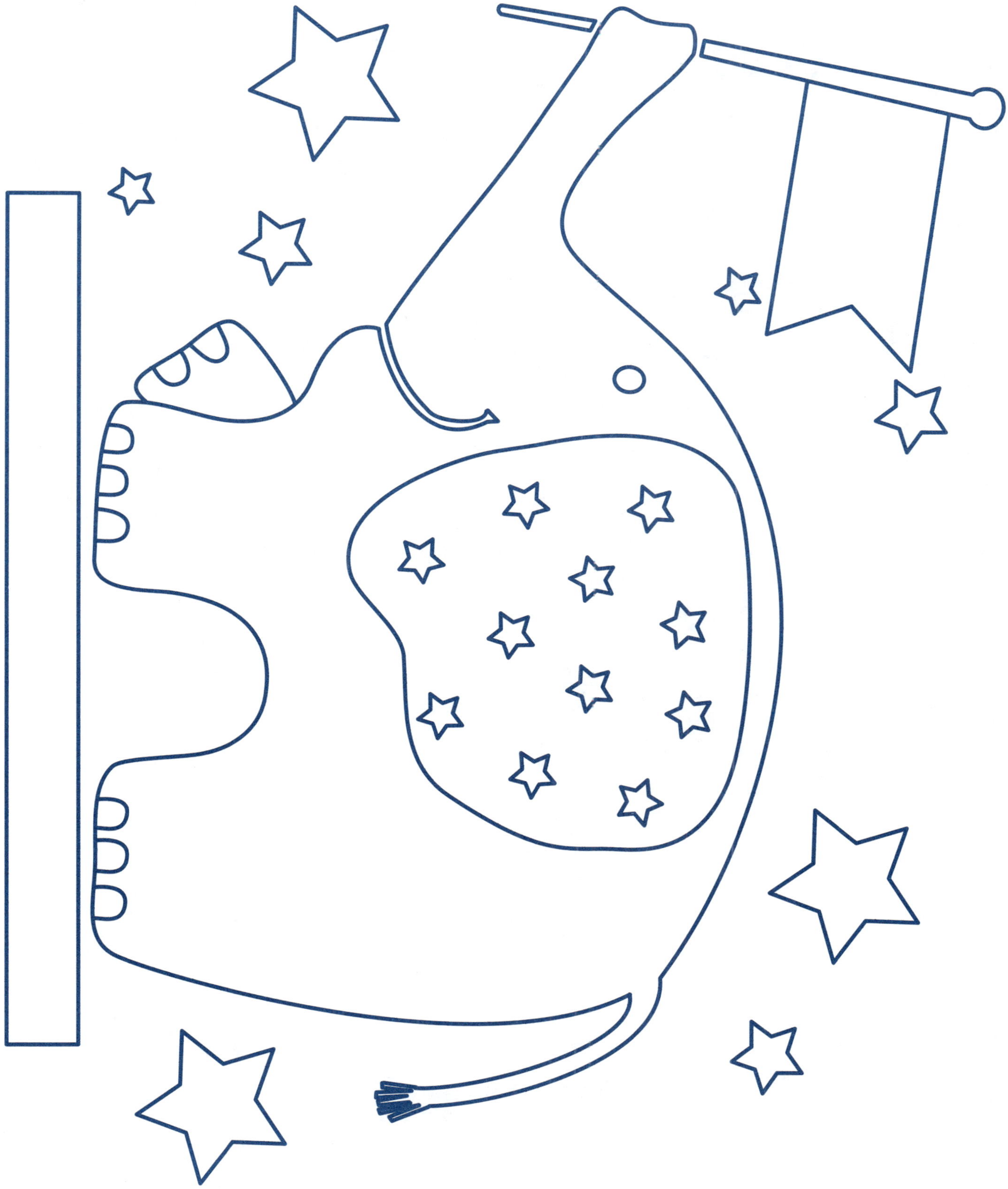

EXTRA! EXTRA!

Paint one or both of these cute bears, then glue on wiggle eyes, a pom-pom nose, and finish by sewing on buttons and bows.

Test Transfer

Extra! Extra!

Make this hippo into a ballerina by adding a tutu of gathered lace and a perky bow. Scattered jewels and a length of lace around the bottom completes the shirt.

Extra! Extra!

Replace the triangles of this design with colorful triangular buttons.

EXTRA! EXTRA!

Add ribbon and star buttons to the box and give the seal a pom-pom nose.

EXTRA! EXTRA!
Use thick outlines of dimensional paint to outline this tiger, then sew on buttons for eyes.

Extra! Extra!

Sew on folded lengths of ribbon to add dimension to this giraffe's mane and glue on square jewels for sparkly eyes.

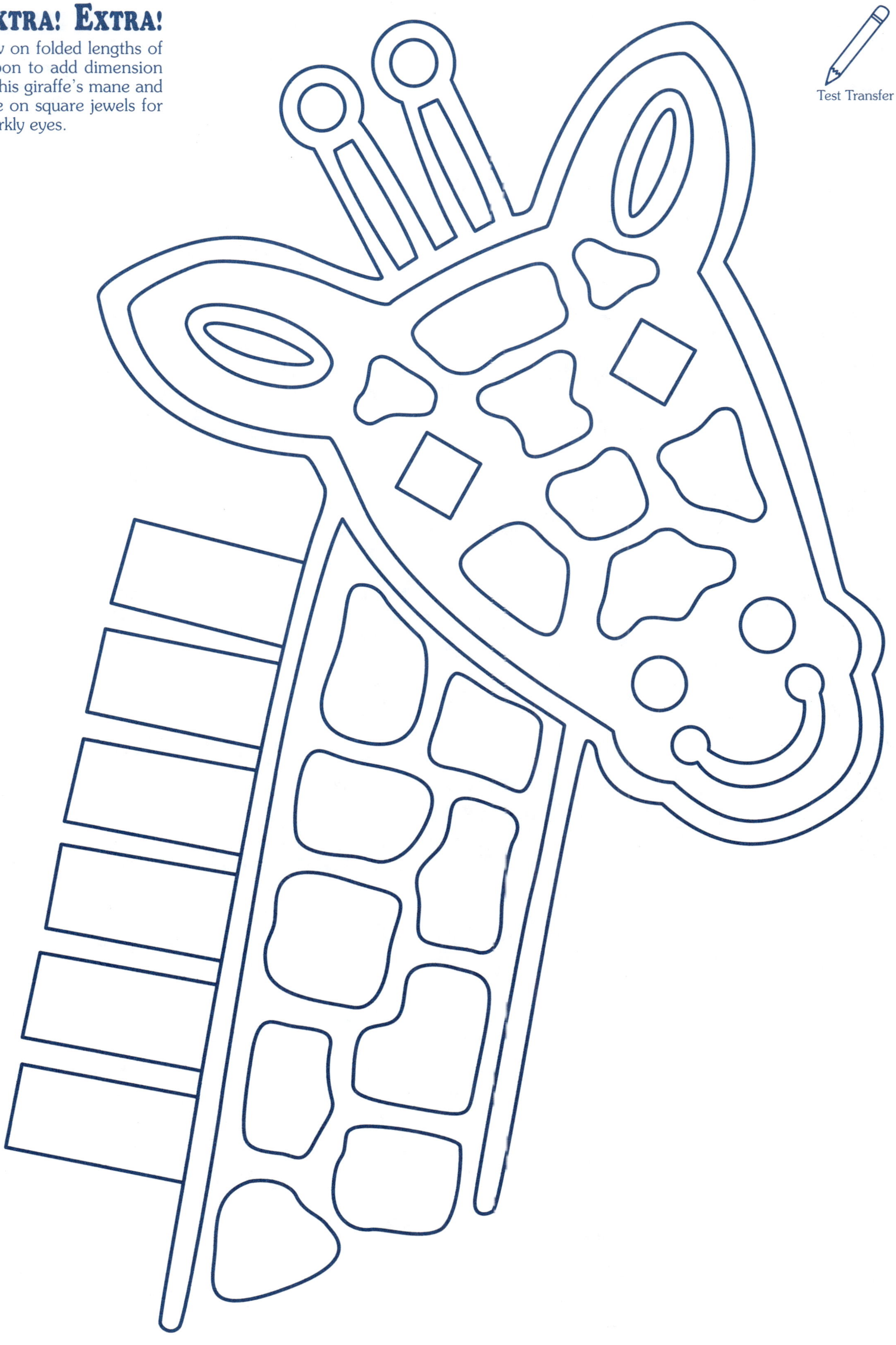

Extra! Extra!

Sew on folded ribbon for the zebra's mane and add beaded trim to the bottom of your shirt.

Test Transfer

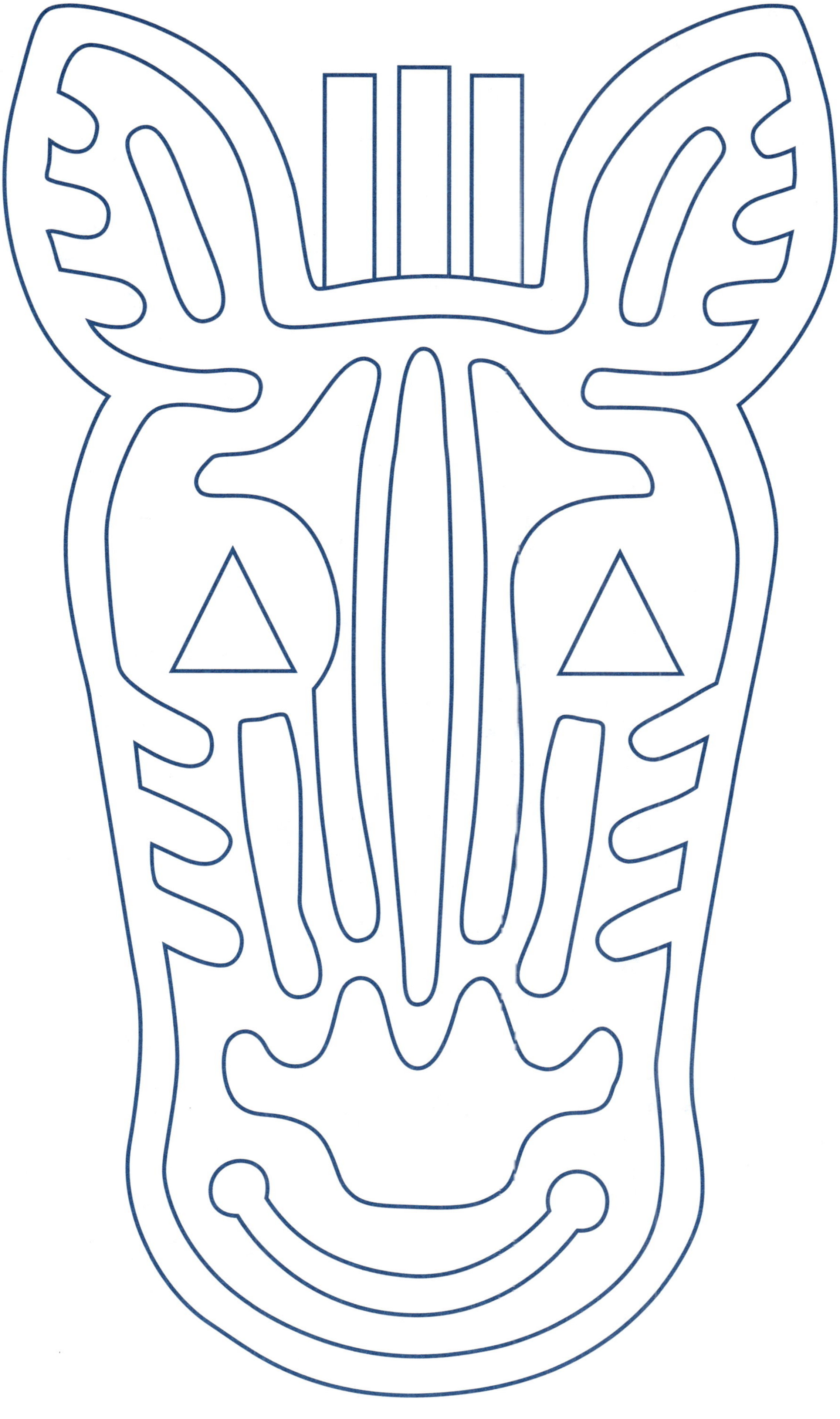

Extra! Extra!

Add glitter highlights, tiny button knobs, and star charms to this musical instrument.

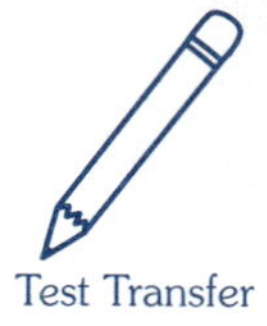

Test Transfer

EXTRA! EXTRA!

Use sequin confetti, dimensional paint keys and notes, and glitter paints to tell the world of your love for music.

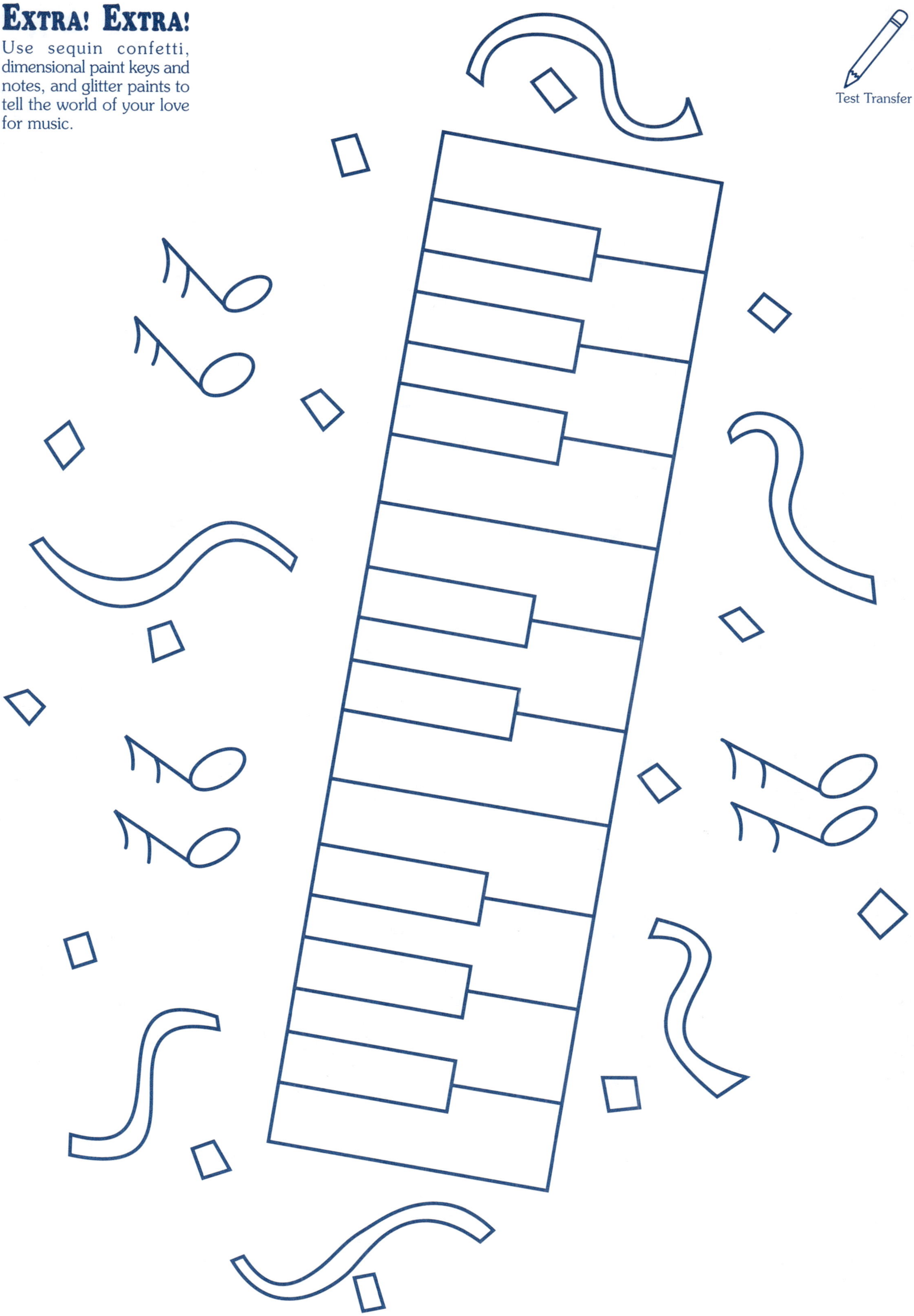

Extra! Extra!

Add brightly colored ribbon and studs for the keys and pom-poms at the end of the sticks to add dimension to this xylophone.

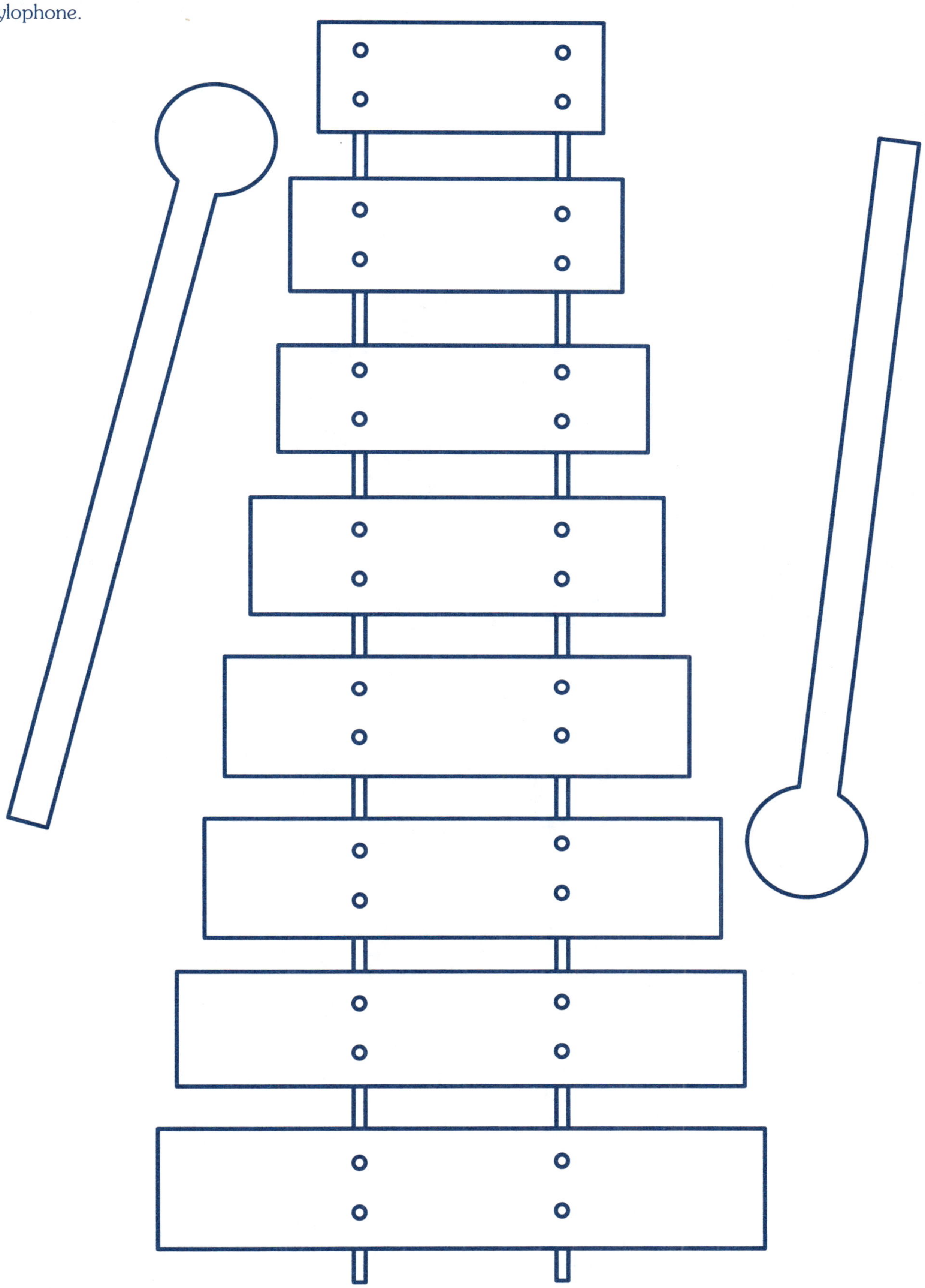

EXTRA! EXTRA!

Replace the road with ribbon, the hubcaps with silver buttons, and the emergency light with a shiny jewel.

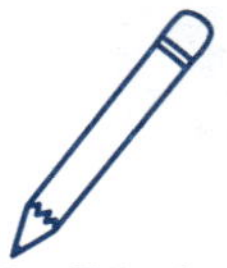

EXTRA! EXTRA!

Replace the border with ribbon and add a touch of glitter to the light and star.

Test Transfer

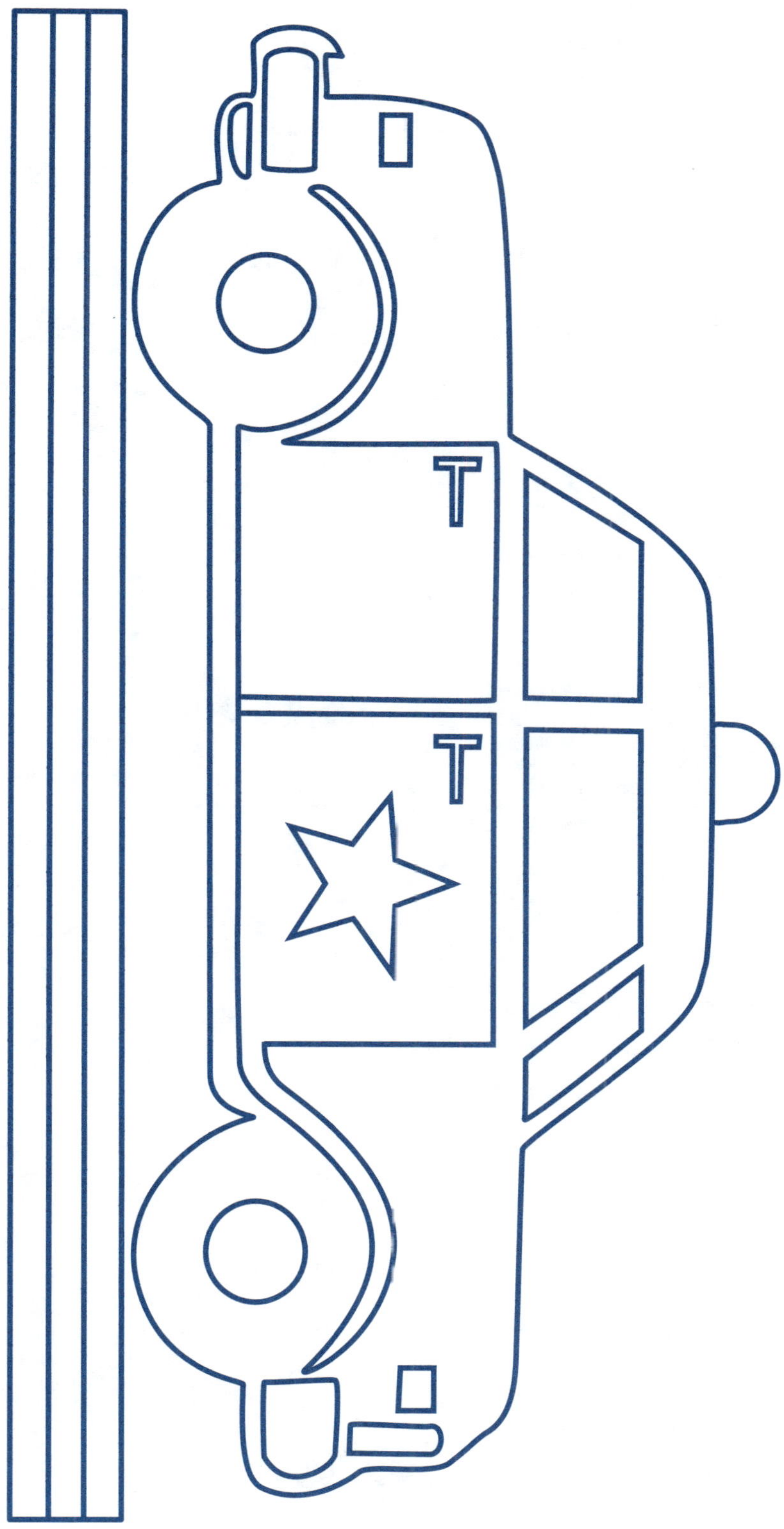

EXTRA! EXTRA!

Use checkerboard ribbon for the flags, ribbon for the stripes on the car, and buttons for wheels. Add a striped ribbon for a road beneath the car and you're off!

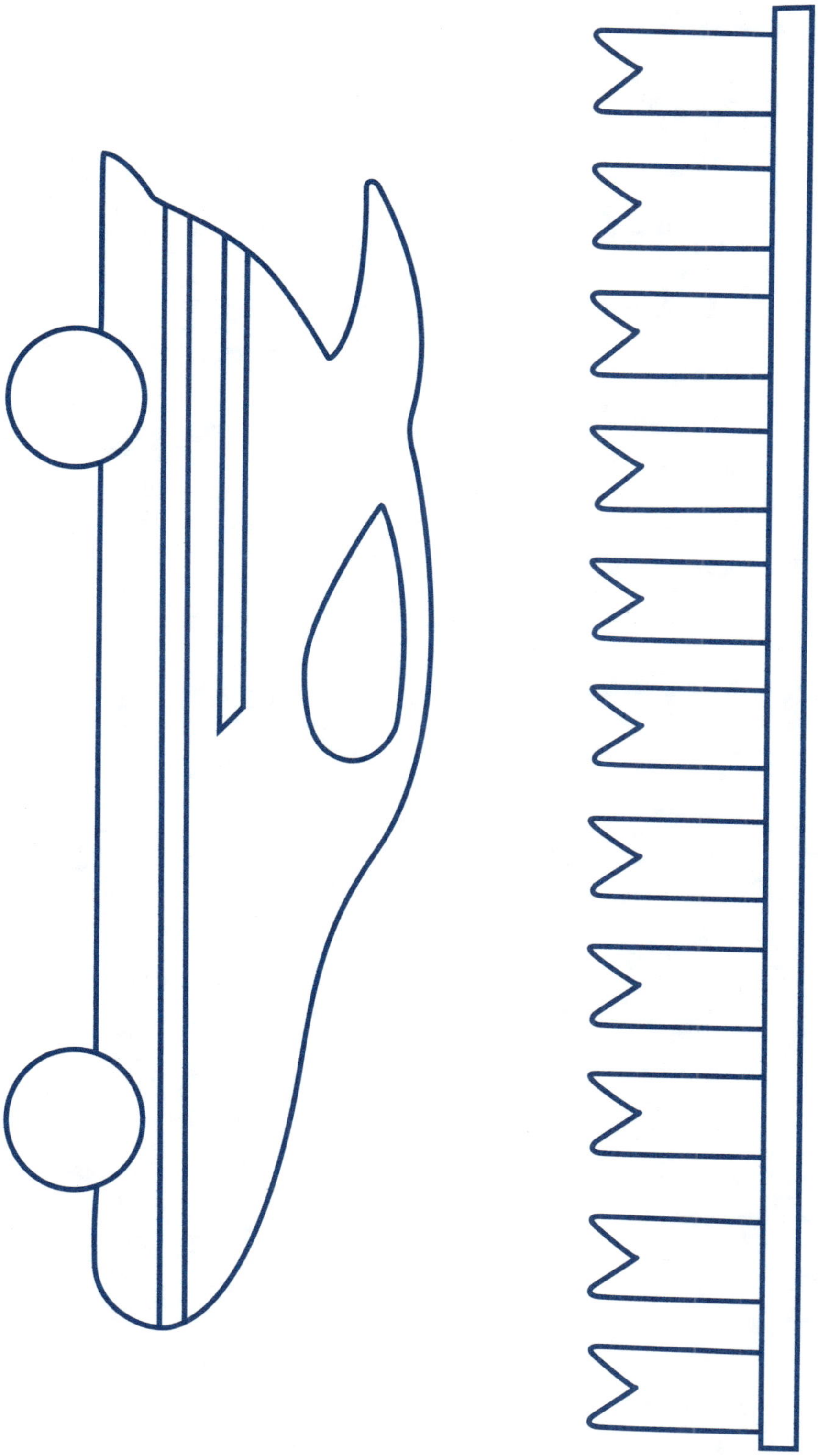

Test Transfer

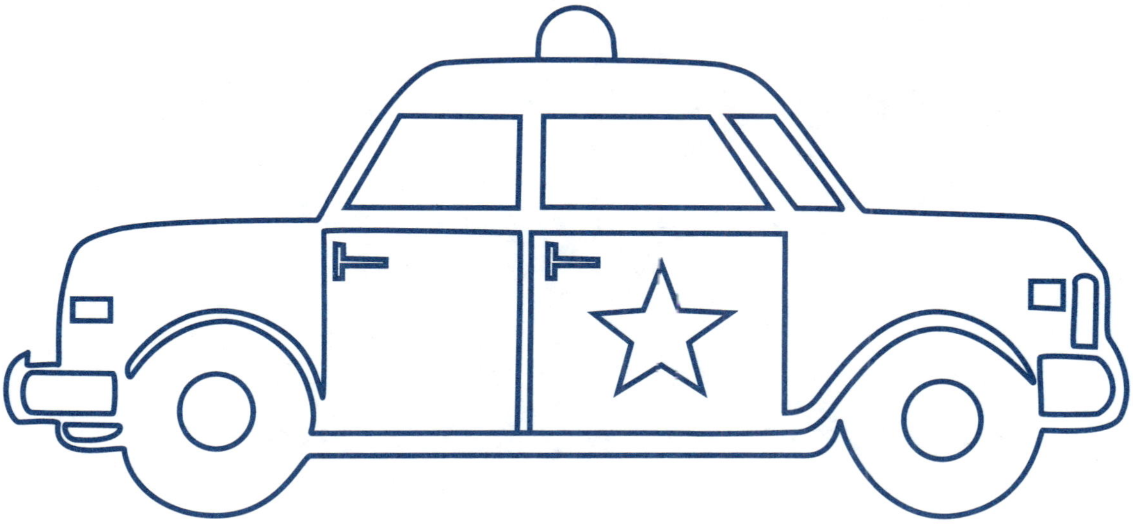

Extra! Extra!

Hop on the bus with buttons and jewels for lights and a ribbon bumper.

Extra! Extra!

Use a colorful ribbon for the border and buttons for the wheels on this locomotive. For an added touch, sponge paint puffs of smoke.

Test Transfer

Extra! Extra!

Replace the flag and hull with ribbon, then add rickrack waves and nautical star buttons. A big button makes a cheery sun.

Extra! Extra!

Use different colors of ribbon for the boat, then add buttons for the portholes and jumbo rickrack for the waves.

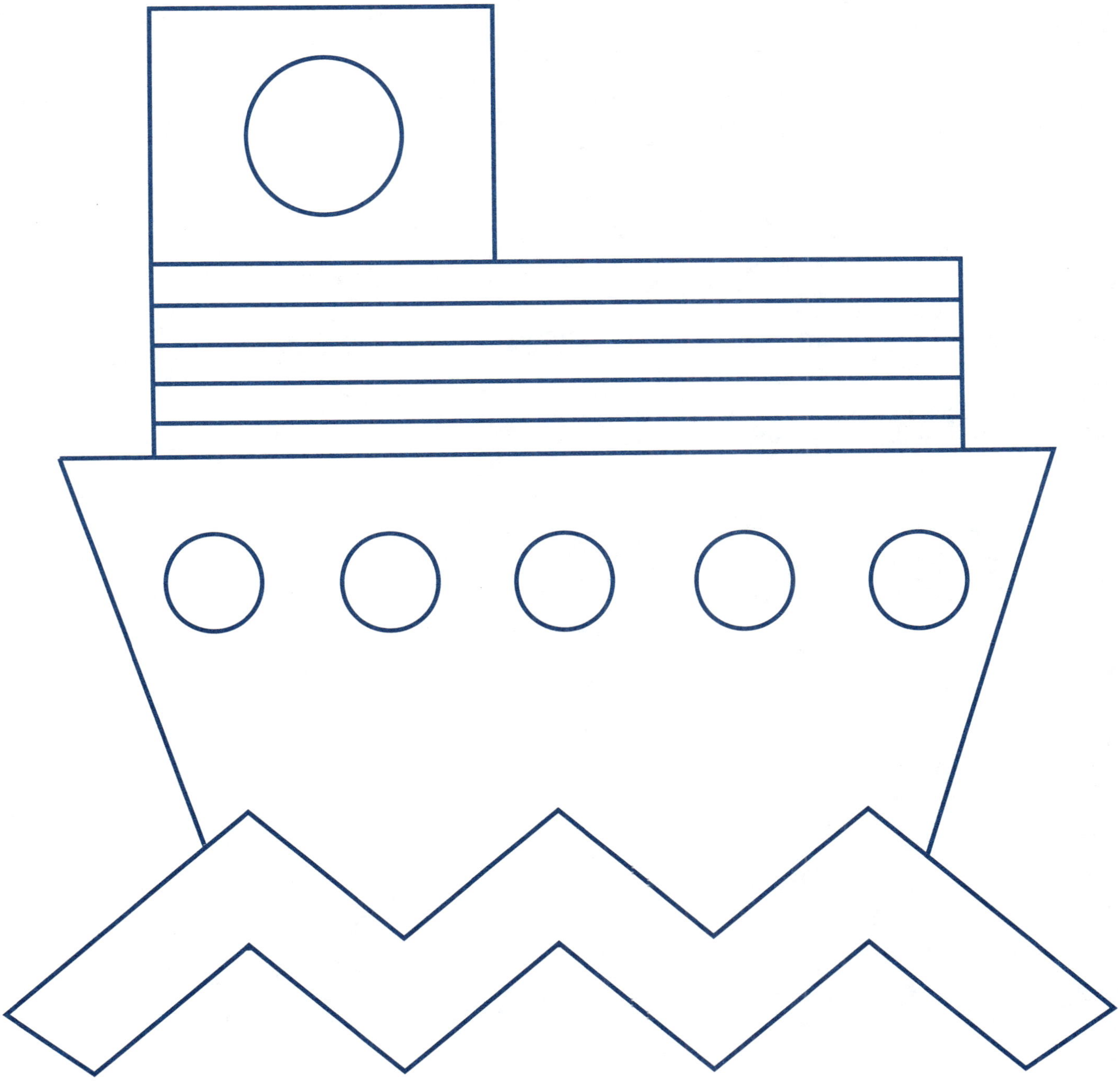

Extra! Extra!

Use the alphabets on the following pages to personalize or add a saying to any of the designs.

Test Transfer

1 2 3 4 5 6 7 8 9 0

a b c d e f g h i j k l

m n o p q r s t u v w x y z

A B C D E

F G H I J K

L M N O P

Q R S T U

V W X Y Z